INSIGHT POCKET GUIDES

BarbaDOS

CW00323669

APA PUBLICATIONS
Part of the Langenscheidt Publishing Group

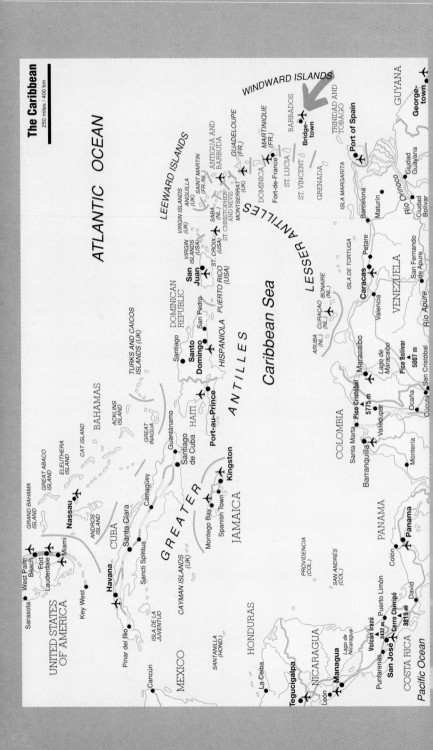

The Caribbean

250 miles / 400 km

WINDWARD ISLANDS

ATLANTIC OCEAN

UNITED STATES OF AMERICA

Sarasota
West Palm Beach
Fort Lauderdale
Miami
Key West

MEXICO

Cancún

BAHAMAS

GRAND BAHAMA ISLAND
GREAT ABACO ISLAND
ELEUTHERA ISLAND
Nassau
ANDROS ISLAND
CAT ISLAND
ACKLINS ISLAND
GREAT INAGUA

TURKS AND CAICOS ISLANDS (UK)

Pinar del Río

Havana

CUBA

ISLA DE LA JUVENTUD

Santa Clara
Sancti Spíritus
Camagüey

CAYMAN ISLANDS (UK)

Santiago de Cuba
Guantánamo

HAITI

Port-au-Prince

DOMINICAN REPUBLIC

Santiago

Santo Domingo

San Pedro

HISPANIOLA

PUERTO RICO (USA)

San Juan

VIRGIN ISLANDS (UK)
VIRGIN ISLANDS (USA)
ST. CROIX (USA)

ANGUILLA (UK)
SAINT MARTIN (FR./NL.)
SABA (NL.)
ST. CHRISTOPHER AND NEVIS
MONTSERRAT (UK)

LEEWARD ISLANDS

ANTIGUA AND BARBUDA

GUADELOUPE (FR.)

DOMINICA

MARTINIQUE (FR.)

Fort-de-France

ST. LUCIA

ST. VINCENT

GRENADA

BARBADOS

Bridge-town

TRINIDAD AND TOBAGO

Port of Spain

GREATER ANTILLES

JAMAICA

Montego Bay
Spanish Town
Kingston

Caribbean Sea

LESSER ANTILLES

PROVIDENCIA (COL.)

SAN ANDRÉS (COL.)

SANTANILLA (HOND.)

HONDURAS

La Ceiba

Tegucigalpa

NICARAGUA

León
Managua

Lago de Nicaragua

COSTA RICA

Puntarenas
San José
Volcán Irazú 3432 m
Cerro Chirripó 3819 m
Puerto Limón

David

PANAMA

Colón
Panama

COLOMBIA

Santa Marta
Barranquilla
Cartagena
Montería
Valledupar
Ocaña
Cúcuta
San Cristóbal
Pico Cristóbal 5775 m
Pico Bolívar 5007 m
Maracaibo
Lago de Maracaibo

ARUBA (NL.)
CURAÇAO (NL.)
BONAIRE (NL.)

ISLA DE TORTUGA

ISLA MARGARITA

VENEZUELA

Caracas
Barcelona
Petare
Valencia
Maturín
Ciudad Guayana
Ciudad Bolívar
Río Orinoco
San Fernando de Apure
Río Apure

GUYANA

George-town

Pacific Ocean

Welcome!

This guidebook combines the interests and enthusiasms of two of the world's best-known information providers: Insight Guides, who have set the standard for visual travel guides since 1970, and Discovery Channel, the world's premier source of non-fiction television programming.

In these pages *Insight Guides'* correspondent in Barbados, Roxan Kinas, has devised a range of tailor-made itineraries to show visitors the best of the island during a stay of about two weeks. Eleven itineraries, beginning with the capital Bridgetown on the west coast and then working around the island in a clockwise direction, link the main sights and beauty spots. She pays due attention to the celebrated west coast, where royalty rubs shoulders with movies stars, and to the bustling south coast, but she also explores the island's quieter side, where donkey carts laden with fresh hay cluck slowly down narrow roads and spectacular east coast beaches can be enjoyed in solitude. Supporting the itineraries are chapters on history and culture, shopping, eating out, nightlife and festivals, and a fact-packed practical information section, which includes a selection of recommended hotels.

Roxan Kinas is a writer, natural life photographer and public relations consultant who has lived and worked on Barbados for over 20 years. As well as writing for regional publications, such as Caribbean Week and BWee Beat, she produces feature articles about Barbados and the Eastern Caribbean islands for the North American press.

C O N T E N T S

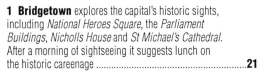

*Pages 2/3:
Where life's
a beach*

Pages 8/9: Independence Day parade

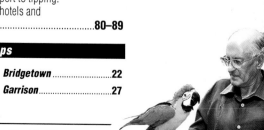

HISTORY & CULTURE

When the British ship *William and John* landed at Holetown on February 17, 1627, no one was there to greet the 80 passengers who came ashore to settle and claim the island for England. Yet they were far from the first to land or even dwell on this wild and densely wooded land. Though the island lies just beyond the main trade and exploration routes of the time and had been bypassed by major explorers, many vessels had managed to stumble across it.

Long before that the south and west coasts were bustling with Amerindian life. Until recently it was assumed that the first inhabitants arrived from the Orinoco Valley around AD300. However, recent archeological finds at sites such as Heywoods and Port St Charles prove the island was a permanent settlement as early as 2000 BC. The island's 75 archeological sites suggest that Amerindian settlements existed up to AD1500, after which they disappeared. The reason for this is still unclear: the Indians could have been forced into slavery by the Spanish; wiped out by European diseases; over-farming or another tribe could have driven them from the island.

In the early 1500s Spanish and Portuguese ships prowled the region. Either by accident or design, ships from these nations passed through and mapped the island under several names, most notably Las Barbudos, which loosely translates as 'the bearded ones.' Whether these 'bearded ones' were trees (bearded fig) or people (bearded Indians) is speculation.

It was the British who settled the island and stayed. Barbados is unique in the region for having enjoyed a peaceful, unbroken relationship with its colonial parent until its independence on

Carib Indians

November 30, 1966. The island also boasts the oldest parliamentary system after Britain and Bermuda in the Commonwealth of Nations. British influence peppers the island in village names, etiquette and lifestyle, but it is marinated in a rich African heritage. The mingling of these two influences gives the island a character unlike any other.

The Road to Sugar

By 1629 the island population had ballooned to 1,800, but thanks to drought and lawlessness a period known as the 'Starving Time' set in. The island's unpopular governor, Henry Hawley, was replaced by Sir William Tuft, but Hawley returned to power soon after. When his draconian methods nearly lost him the post a second time, Hawley changed his hard-line approach and the result was the establishment of the House of Assembly in 1639.

Barbados soon enjoyed prosperity based on tobacco and cotton. The primary labor pool for this work was drawn from white indentured servants, commonly called 'Red Legs,' who had come from England, Ireland and Scotland to escape political persecution or imprisonment. Some were condemned criminals, but others were from the higher echelons of British society, exiled in Barbados for their political beliefs. The indentured period was usually five or seven years, after which they would be given a small sum of money or a piece of land to make a new start.

Planting cane

The beginning of the English Civil War in 1642 brought unexpected benefits to Barbados. The 'Mother Country' turned her attention away from the colonies, and Barbados began trading with the Dutch, who were to play a pivotal role in the island's development. The war also brought a more refined breed of settler, who set about replicating the lifestyle and economic prosperity enjoyed in England. It was at this time that Barbados became known as 'Little England.'

When the quality of the island's tobacco failed to compete in the world market and the supply of white indentured servants began to dry up, Barbados turned to sugar. The first canes arrived from Brazil in 1637 and local planters began manufacturing sugar with the help of the Dutch, who supplied canes, mill technology as well as West African slaves for this labor-intensive crop. It was soon discovered that a potent drink could be made from fermented molasses, a by-product in the sugar-making process. These were the crude beginnings of the rum industry that exists today.

11

A member of the 'plantocracy'

The influx of cultured British settlers coupled with a vast new labor pool and a slow mastery of the art of sugar production ushered in a period of unprecedented prosperity. From 1651 until the early 1700s Barbados was said to be the most prosperous island of the British West Indies, and one of the most successful British colony islands in the world.

A new 'plantocracy' class reigned. Lavish plantations were designed after the popular Jacobean and Georgian styles (examples of which remain today), and the ruling class led an opulent, sometimes decadent lifestyle, boasting monumental homes and furnishings. Gambling was a favorite pastime that often lost an owner his entire plantation. Journals and diaries of that period report lavish hospitality that surpassed what one might expect in Britain.

Slavery

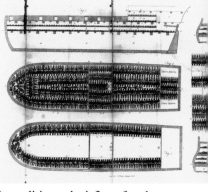

By 1712 Barbados had close to 42,000 slaves. Despite the oppression and severe hardships, runaway and rebellious elements remained small compared with other islands. Several thwarted uprisings took place in the late 1600s, but on such a small island almost completely planted with canes and other crops there was nowhere to run.

But by the end of the 18th century the combination of harsh conditions, the influx of replacement slaves less resigned to a life of unrelenting hardship, and the advent of 'free-colored people' (freed slaves) added to a growing air of dissent. Outside Barbados the great reform movement was building and after the British parliament's 1807 abolition of the slave trade, freedom was on the horizon.

In 1816 free mulatto Washington Francklyn masterminded a slave revolt. Among the slave leaders was the now famous Bussa, a headman at Bayley's Plantation. Cane fires set in St Philip signaled the start of the revolt and burned their way into neighboring parishes.

The slaves stood little chance against regiment of local militia. In the end one-fifth of the island's crop was razed, property was destroyed, 176 slaves died fighting and another 214 were executed. Francklyn was among those executed and Bussa died in battle. It took another 22 years of stubborn resistance by the planters, however, before slavery was finally abolished in 1838.

Though imported African slaves came primarily from West Africa, language barriers and diverse cultural backgrounds made it difficult for them to carry on their traditions on Barbados. Among the elements of African culture that did survive the centuries are a belief in *obeah*, or magic, a smattering of words, and distinct African influences in diet and music.

Riots, Reforms and Independence

By the start of the 20th century, Barbados was feeling the crush of a high and ever increasing population, and the austere economic conditions that ensued combined with the lack of union or constitutional representation of the general labor force led, in 1937, to riots. On July 26, 1937 workers amassed in Bridgetown for a meeting to discuss the deportation of Trinidadian union agitator Clement Payne. The situation escalated out of control, and soon Bridgetown was in a shambles. Rural areas quickly caught wind of the disorder and followed suit, resulting in 14 deaths, many injuries, hundreds of arrests and wide-scale damage to property.

The incident led to the launch, in 1938, of the Barbados Progressive League, later to become the Barbados Labour Party (BLP). Under the leadership of Oxford-educated barrister and journalist Grantley Adams (later Sir), within two years of its formation the party had won five parliamentary seats. Again under Adams' leadership, the Barbados Workers' Union was formed, leading to a virtual revolution in employment and living conditions, as well as important constitutional and educational reforms.

Sir Grantley Adams

A highly qualified professional, Sir Grantley came to be known as the leader of the island's 'social revolution,' working tirelessly to build the labor movement both at home and in the wider region. By 1958 the Cabinet system was instituted with Grantley becoming the island's first premier.

One of the Labour Party's members elected in 1951 was left-wing Errol Walton Barrow. After crossing swords with Adams over

13

labor and other issues, Barrow broke away from the party and in 1955 formed the Democratic Labour Party (DLP). Later in a stunning 1961 election victory, he became the nation's leader.

Errol Barrow, today a national hero, was responsible for leading Barbados to Independence in 1966. He introduced free education, launched the still-active school meals program and significantly improved the wages and working conditions of public workers.

Then in 1976 a young upstart usurped Barrow in an overwhelming election defeat. The young leader was J.M.G.M (Tom) Adams, the

son of the late Sir Grantley. But Barrow remained in politics, winning the election again in 1986, and leading the nation until his death in June the following year.

Barrow was succeeded by Lloyd Erskine Sandiford who enjoyed seven years in power. However the nation grew increasingly disheartened in the face of a faltering economy. At the next election in 1994 the Barbados Labour Party was returned, led by the current Prime Minister the Rt Hon. Owen Arthur, heralding a new period of optimism. His shrewd management has restored faith in the economy and has attracted significant foreign investment, ushering in a new era of prosperity.

Tourism thrives winter and summer

Tourism versus Agriculture

Tourism in Barbados dates back to the 1700s when visitors came for the salubrious climate. In 1751 George Washington accompanied his tubercular brother Lawrence to the island, the only occasion he left his homeland in his whole life. Later, in the first half of the 20th century, Barbados became a popular long-stay winter destination for very wealthy British visitors, many of whom built lavish homes along the west coast. Today tourism is the island's primary revenue earner, bringing close to 500,000 visitors each year. In the 1990s the cruise ship industry became particularly significant.

But even so Barbados remains an agricultural nation, with a booming cut-flower industry and self-sufficiency in many foodstuffs.

The history of sugar production on Barbados is one of peaks and troughs. The industry has been challenged by competing demands for land and by relatively high labor costs. But sugar remains the principal agricultural crop and a significant foreign exchange earner.

Hard Times Celebrated

The island's biggest festival, Crop Over, traces its roots back to the plantation era, when the end of the crop represented both the end of hard work and the start of hard times. It was a plantation event, a day for role reversal and frolic. As the last procession of carts made their way into the mill yard, a laborer would beat a make-shift gong, announcing the crop over.

The draft animals and carts were decorated with flowers and the canes themselves tied with bright bandannas. The workers joined the procession, all wearing flowers in their headgear. One cart would carry a cane effigy of 'Mr Harding' (symbolizing hard times and the cruel gang-drivers) which was burned at the end of the festivities. (The 'Mr Harding' element was dropped from modern-day festivities some years ago.) After the parade around the yard, a speech was made by a favored worker followed by a reply by the owner or manager. Festivities were then punctuated by lavish spreads of food and drink, usually rum, along with games and contests, including the now dying art of 'stick-licking' (stick fighting), dancing and singing. Music was a key element.

Today an entire month of activities is devoted to the festival. Many of the original elements, such as the donkey cart parade and the ceremonial delivery of the last canes, remain in some form. Other elements, including calypso tents and competitions, evolved in the 1970s, when Crop Over (starting in July) was revived after a 30-year hiatus.

During the festival virtually every form of music the island has to offer is heard, including Tuk, a fusion of British marching music and African rhythms. Roving Tuk bands wend their way through the crowds playing the kettle drum, bass drum and penny whistle in a unique format and cadence, beginning with a slow waltz, moving into a marching rhythm and concluding in a frenetic African beat.

Celebrating Crop Over

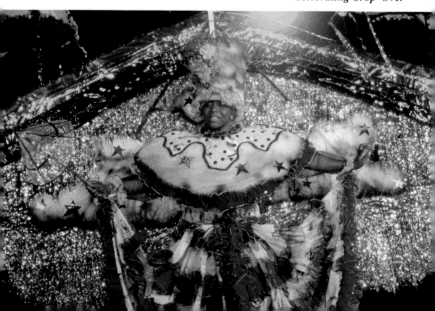

Typical chattel house

The Chattel House

An historical aspect of Barbados still very apparent today is the chattel house, the quaint, colorfully painted houses found in rows in villages throughout the island.

Chattel means 'movable possession', and the buildings originated when newly emancipated slaves were required to provide their own housing while working on the plantations. They needed homes that could be taken apart, moved and reassembled all in one day. Such housing was located on plantation land in an area known as a 'tenantry,' where the soil level was too shallow for cultivation.

The houses were made from pine and were of fixed dimensions, such as 8 x 16ft (2.4 x 4.9m), 10 x 20ft (3 x 6m) or 9 x 12ft (2.7 x 3.7m), based on pre-cut lengths imported from North America. Each unit was divided into a minimum of nine sections; four sides, a floor, two gables, two roof sections, and interior partitions. While the original chattel houses looked similar to the ones built today, the early ones were in fact cruder, having first thatched roofs, later shingles, and after the 1955 Hurricane Janet galvanized roofing.

Their construction was of mortise and tenon style, where frame and joints fitted into one another. This made the building stronger against the elements and more easily dismantled. It also allowed the owner to expand at the back and/or front as the family grew or came into more money.

The houses were set on coral stone blocks for easy moving and to give them added elevation for greater privacy, protection from flooding and better floorboard ventilation. This method of propping the houses is still seen island-wide. Always symmetrical in appearance, they had a front door in the center with a window to each side. Variety came in the type of doors and windows used, and the color.

The Tenantry Act of 1981 allowed chattel house owners to purchase the land on which they stood at a low rate. Subsequent to this, a more permanent bungalow-style house began to emerge, with cement foundations and walls.

The chattel house remains a beautiful and indigenous part of the Barbadian culture, their riot of colors painting the countryside with a distinctive flourish.

Historical Highlights

2000BC Barbados is discovered by Amerindians from the Orinoco Basin.

200BC Amerindians of the Saladoid period make the first permanent settlements along the south coast, Heywoods, Hillcrest and Bathsheba.

AD800 New Amerindian settlements develop in the Troumassoid period.

1200 Amerindian population explosion with over 60 sites on the coast.

1500 The Spaniards land on Barbados; Amerindians are wiped out.

1536 A Portuguese ship lands and finds the island uninhabited.

1625 The first English ship, *The Olive*, stumbles onto Barbados, landing at what will become Holetown. The newcomers claim the island for James I of England.

1627 Barbados officially becomes an English possession with the landing of the *William and John* containing 80 settlers.

1628 The capital city, Bridgetown, is founded.

1637 The first sugar cane plants are imported from Brazil.

1639 The House of Assembly is established in Bridgetown.

1642 Sugar is manufactured for the first time, rum – produced from molasses – is discovered as a by-product.

1644 West African slaves begin arriving in vast numbers to support the island's new labor-intensive sugar industry.

1675 The first slave uprising is thwarted, resulting in the execution of 17 ringleaders.

1745 Barbados becomes the first British colony to establish an institution of higher learning with the opening of Codrington College.

1766 Bridgetown is destroyed by fire.

1780 A hurricane almost destroys the entire island and its crops.

1816 The famous 'Bussa' slave revolt results in considerable crop and property damage and the death of almost 400 slaves.

1831 A law is passed granting free colored people legal equality with whites. The 'Great Hurricane' devastates the island.

1834 The Emancipation Act is enacted, launching the apprenticeship system in anticipation of granting emancipation to all slaves.

1838 Slavery is abolished.

1884 A Franchise Act intending to widen the voting base comes into effect. It lowers voter qualifications to persons earning a salary of £50 a year among other stipulations.

1902 An outbreak of smallpox leads to death, quarantine and isolation of the island.

1937 Labor riots sparked by harsh economic conditions break out in Bridgetown and the countryside.

1938 The island's first labor organization, the Barbados Progressive League, is launched under the leadership of (Sir) Grantley Adams. Soon after, he is elected President.

1954 The Vestry system of local government is replaced by ministerial administration; Grantley Adams becomes the island's first premier.

1961 The Democratic Labour Party wins its first election under the leadership of Errol Barrow.

1966 Barbados becomes an independent nation.

1976 Under the leadership of Tom Adams, son of Grantley Adams, the Barbados Labour Party wins the general election and moves the island into a period of economic reform and increasing tourism.

1974 The near-extinct sugar crop festival, Crop Over, is revived.

1979 The airport opens with a long runway to accommodate Concorde.

1985 The Ministry of Tourism is established.

1989 Barbados celebrates 350 years of unbroken parliamentary rule.

1996 Barbados and other Caribbean community (Caricom) nations renew debate on the launch of a Caribbean Court of Appeal to replace the existing appeal system of the British Privy Council (Judicial Committee).

1998 Ten Barbadian National Heroes are announced.

1999 Trafalgar Square, Bridgetown is renamed National Heroes Square.

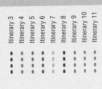

Barbados

3 km / 1.8 miles

- ● ● ● Itinerary 3
- ● ● ● Itinerary 4
- ● ● ● Itinerary 5
- ● ● ● Itinerary 6
- ● ● ● Itinerary 7
- ● ● ● Itinerary 8
- ● ● ● Itinerary 9
- ● ● ● Itinerary 10
- ● ● ● Itinerary 11

Day Itineraries

Each of Barbados' 11 parishes offers something special, and in this series of itineraries I have divided the island into regions, loosely using the parishes as guidelines.

The northeast, southeast and central areas include the main sights ranging from historic buildings to specialty parks, while the south and west coasts are highly developed and offer the best shopping. The central areas are lusher and more obviously scenic than the flatter coastal areas, but the latter offer an unsullied rugged beauty that is also appealing.

What one person finds intriguing and worth a few hours' visit, another may consider less exciting. Therefore, many of the trips include several diverse attractions and you will probably decide to choose whichever interests you most.

Though small, Barbados is a veritable maze of unmarked winding roads. Do not get frustrated if you find yourself lost after mistaking a main road for a secondary one, or if you make a wrong

West coast idyll

turn. Just relax and consider it part of the fun of exploring the island. Most Bajans are friendly and helpful and will point you in the right direction.

We will be using the 'ABC' Highway as the starting point for our tours. This highway stretches from the airport to the edge of St James in the west. Here the road parts, extending either to the coast (ABC continuation) or inland on Highway 2A to the north in St Peter. The highway is interrupted by roundabouts, which we will use to start and end our tours. Once you have located the best route to get onto the 'ABC,' use that to begin your tours.

Taking a view on life

Several of the historic properties on the itineraries are owned, operated or supported by the island's heritage organization, the Barbados National Trust (BNT). If you plan to visit several of these, you may want to obtain a Heritage Passport from the Trust, which gives discounted admission to a range of properties depending on the 'passport' you select. Such passports also offer discounts at shops and other attractions as well as on Trust publications and videos (for details, tel: 436-9033). The Trust also has reciprocal agreements with other heritage organizations around the world so you may find joining the Trust will bring you even greater savings.

1. Bridgetown

A morning walking tour of Bridgetown's historic sights. Lunch along the careenage and an afternoon shopping. If you plan to shop duty free don't forget your passport and ticket. Guard your belongings carefully while in the city.

—For this tour you can take a bus or van into Bridgetown then walk around the sights. If you intend to drive and are arriving from the south coast, park in Independence Square car park and walk across the bridge into Bridgetown. West coast visitors enter Bridgetown from Spring Garden Highway then Fontabelle, and should park in city center car park, a block off Broad Street—

Bridgetown was established in 1628, but it was not the most favorable site to found a city for the nearby sea and swamp guaranteed episodes of disease and flooding. Richard Ligon in his book *True & Exact History of Barbadoes* (1657) noted: 'A town ill situate; for if they had considered health, as they did conveniency, they would never have set it there...But, one house being set up, another was erected, and so a third, and a fourth, till at last it came to take the name of a Town.' Despite the flooding and poor sanitation, the town grew.

Nelson surveys Heroes Square

The capital's name is traditionally believed to come from a primitive Amerindian bridge spanning the waterway. Early deeds mention 'The Indian Bridge,' 'The Indian Bridgetown' and 'The Bridge.' By 1660, St Michael's Town became the favored name, and was in use into the 19th century. The main streets of Bridgetown were laid out by surveyor John Swan, and the street behind Broad Street was later named after him.

Broad Street (the main drag) was originally a market area called Cheapside. Today, only the far western end and the market are known by that name. In the late 1600s it was called the Exchange or Exchange Street because the Merchants' Exchange was situated here. By the early 1700s it had become Broad Street.

At the top of Broad Street is **National Heroes Square**. Formerly known as Trafalgar Square, it features a statue of Lord Nelson erected in 1813 – some three decades before London's own Nelson's Column. (The government intends to move the statue to another location.) Plans to raise a statue in Nelson's memory were begun within weeks of his victory and subsequent death at Cape Trafalgar in 1805. In fact, it was a tremendous source of pride to Barbadians, who thought they were the first (in fact they were the

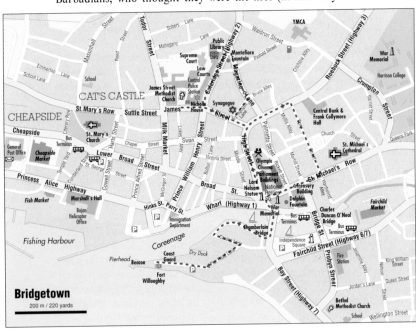

Bridgetown

200 m / 220 yards

third, after Montreal and Birmingham) to raise a monument honoring the military leader. Sculpted from bronze by Sir Richard Westmacott ('the first castor of bronze in the Kingdom'), it is regarded as an excellent likeness of the British admiral.

The land occupied by National Heroes Square was first purchased in 1807 and expanded to its present size in 1826. The fountain, known as the Dolphin Fountain, was erected in 1865 to commemorate the advent of piped water in Bridgetown. The garden itself and the enclosure came slightly later, the earliest work beginning in 1882.

Parliament Buildings

Across from National Heroes Square are the Public Buildings, now called the **Parliament Buildings**. Plans to erect a parliament and public records building were initiated in 1692 after the island's new governor arrived to discover sessions were being held in public houses (taverns), but apart from a brief period (1700–4) when meetings were conducted in the more appropriate State House they continued to be held in public houses, residences and other rented facilities until the Public Buildings were erected in 1871, almost 240 years after parliament was established in Barbados. It took a tragedy to spark action. After a devastating fire in 1860 the Public Buildings Erection Committee acquired plots from what was called the New Burnt District.

The first (West) building was completed in late 1871 and presented to government on January 1, 1872. The East building was completed in 1874, and in 1875 the clock and bells, imported from England, were installed in the East building tower. However, the weight of the tower and its contents was too heavy for the foundations and the building began to sink. In 1884 the clock was taken out and the south tower of the West building was redesigned to hold the clock. Made by B.R. and T. Moore, the eight-day Public Buildings clock even runs while being wound.

The Parliament Buildings are designed in neo-Gothic style, a 19th-century copy of medieval religious architecture. Among the features of note are the stained-glass windows depicting all the British monarchs from James I to Queen Victoria, as well as Oliver Cromwell, the 17th-century Lord Protector. The West wing will house a gallery dedicated to the National Heroes of Barbados.

23

Going next to the **Synagogue**, walk up High Street (northern side of National Heroes Square) then turn onto James Street and walk one block to the tiny alleyway called Synagogue Lane on the right. As you come up this short street, you will see the Synagogue (Monday to Friday 9am–4pm) on the

site of the first Jewish synagogue in the Western hemisphere. Built in 1654, the building was destroyed by the Great Hurricane of 1831. The current building was opened in 1833.

By 1929 there was only one practicing Jew left in Barbados and the building was sold and turned into offices. By the early

The Jewish cemetery

1980s the building had become derelict and a restoration effort was launched by the local Jewish community with assistance from the Barbados National Trust, government and the Caribbean Conservation Association.

Next to the building is the **Jewish cemetery** with graves dating back to 1660. Today the Synagogue is in active use and has received various preservation awards and accolades.

Synagogue Lane leads to Magazine Lane – so named because it was near the site of the Public Magazine, built in 1683 by Simon Cooper, then demolished in 1728 to make room for the Town Hall at the corner of James and Coleridge Streets.

Turn left on Magazine Lane where the most visible sight is **Montefiore Fountain**, a drinking fountain presented to the City of Bridgetown in 1864 by Swan Street businessman John Montefiore in memory of his father, who died in 1854. The father, also named John, was a prominent Bridgetown merchant described in historical archives as a 'free colored.' The fountain's first home was in another section of the city called Beckwith Place, at the corner of Broad and Tudor streets. It was moved to its present site in June 1940. Each side of the fountain is decorated with a marble mythical figure representing one of four attributes: Fortitude ('Look to the End'), Temperance ('Be soberminded'), Patience ('To bear is to conquer') and Justice ('Do wrong to no one').

Across from the fountain is the **Public Library**, opened in 1904 and paid for by the Scottish-American philanthropist Andrew Carnegie. It stands on part of the land that was the prison yard of the Common Gaol. Climb the outside steps of the library and have

a look at the beautiful room and ceiling of the children's library. This is the original ceiling, which has been restored.

Next door is a cluster of buildings, including the **Law Courts** and the **Supreme Court** building, formerly the Town Hall. This edifice was built in 1730 for housing the Legislature, Law Courts and the Common Gaol. While the gaol confined primarily civil and criminal offenders, it occasionally served as a wartime prisoner of war facility as well. Many prisoners were moved to Glendairy Prison on its completion in 1855, and the Town Hall Gaol was closed in 1876.

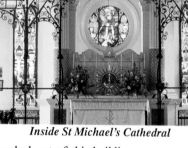
Inside St Michael's Cathedral

Though the Law Courts section of the compound was altered in the 1950s with the addition of a verandah that leads from the Registrar's office to the Central Hall, you can still see the beauty of the building at its eastern end.

To reach **Nicholls House**, considered the oldest surviving building in Bridgetown, walk from the library past the island's first police station to James Street. Nicholls House is on the corner, on the same side of the street as the police station. Reflecting the Dutch influences introduced to Bridgetown during the 17th century, Nicholls House has classic Dutch gabling and an attic door in the center which originally housed a winch for hauling merchandise. The building, now a law office, was named after a father/son team of dentists who worked out of this building from the 1930s for some two decades.

The next sight on the itinerary is St Michael's Cathedral. Go down James Street and turn left at the large intersection to meet Roebuck Street. Follow it to Spry Street, just a block or so ahead on the right. You will see a tall, imposing modern building, which is the **Central Bank of Barbados**. Then you will pass the Masonic Lodge, a large older building which was the first site of Harrison College, and **St Michael's Cathedral** is on your left. The cathedral conducts tours, and you can ask about taking one when you arrive. This is the second Anglican church built on this site. The first, consecrated in 1665, was destroyed by a hurricane in 1780. But even before nature razed it, the building was nearly destroyed by incompetent repair work necessitated by the massive roof span. A new building was erected soon after the hurricane, but it too suffered structural problems. It became a cathedral in 1825 under William Coleridge, one of the West Indies' first Anglican bishops.

Chamberlain Bridge

Time for lunch and a walk along the historic careenage. Continue on to St Michael's Row and turn right. You will see the Fountain Gardens ahead. Go back to the top of Broad Street, cross the Chamberlain Bridge and turn right down into the careenage walkway.

The **Chamberlain Bridge**, formerly known as the 'swing bridge', was renamed after Joseph Chamberlain, the British Colonial Secretary of the late 1800s who was instrumental in salvaging a floundering sugar industry burdened by excessive taxation. In the early days a wooden bridge was built to replace the Indian bridge settlers found when they arrived. Several other versions were erected and subsequently destroyed, mostly by fire, flooding or hurricane. One of many amusing bridge-building episodes occurred in 1751 after the government commissioned John McDonnell to construct a stone bridge in place of the constantly faltering wooden structures. On completion, the wooden scaffolding was dismantled and the bridge immediately collapsed, the stones all tumbling into the channel and blocking it. Having spent £3,595, only to have this albatross fail, the government prosecuted those involved. The bridge today, built in 1872, no longer swings and is closed to traffic.

Walk the length of the careenage (so called because the old wooden ships would be 'careened' or turned on their sides to have their hulls cleaned here) and before the end you will come to the screw

Landing barracudas

dock. Built between 1889 and 1893, this dry dock is a fine example of Victorian engineering and is thought to be the only dock of its kind in the world. An intricate piece of workmanship, it provided respite and repair for ships for almost a century.

You can lunch at the **Rusty Pelican** or **Waterfront Café**. Both are good, reasonably priced eateries, with a scenic view of the harbor. Or walk a bit further out of town to **The Boatyard** for a beachfront setting.

The wharf is also the starting point for a variety of sea adventures including scuba diving, deep-sea fishing and sailing. On the far shore or northern bank of the wharf **Bajan Helicopters** (tel: 431-0069) has exciting 20- and 30-minute flightseeing trips.

On your way back into Bridgetown, you may want to stop off at some boutiques along the wharf front; **Soul Philosophy** and **Colours of de Caribbean** sell good quality clothing and souvenirs.

2. The Garrison

A walking tour around the historic Garrison with stops at the Barbados Gallery of Art and the Barbados Museum. If you go on a Saturday morning you can attend the afternoon horse races at the Savannah.

—This is an introductory tour around the Garrison. If you have a special interest in the history of Barbados, buy 'The Barbados Garrison and its Buildings' (see further reading, page 90), which highlights all the buildings of the old Garrison in detail—

The Garrison is on the southern outskirts of Bridgetown, just off Bay Street. You can get there from Bridgetown or follow Highway 7. From either direction, turn into Bush Hill (opposite the Barbados Light & Power Company building). At the first monument turn right and drive the few yards to the cannons. You can park anywhere along here and walk around the Garrison. If it is a race day, park so that

A day at the races

you will not get hemmed in when the crowds arrive.

There are 60 to 70 Garrison buildings in all. While many of these are now in private or government use, efforts are underway to bring many back to their original appearance, as well as to use the St Ann's Fort compound (now occupied by the Defense Force) to house collections of important artifacts including the National Cannon collection.

This was the first garrison in the West Indies and probably in North America. Barbados had some 50 forts and batteries around the island and was well fortified from the 1600s, first by the Barbados militia, then by the British Army.

A litany of events caused the people of Barbados to feel the need for fortifications. The first was around 1650, when Needham's Fort (soon after named Charles Fort) was constructed at Needham's Point to stave off a landing

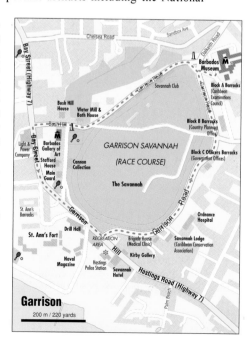

Garrison

200 m / 220 yards

by the Commonwealth Expedition under Oliver Cromwell's rule. Though the fort was originally made from branch bundles it apparently served them well, for it was action from this fort that fended off invasion by a Dutch fleet in 1665.

St Ann's Fort was built after war with France started in 1688. Originally intended to be a 'little castle or detached bastion' to support Fort Charles, it was ultimately built as a 1½-acre (0.6-hectare) stone wall hexagon to the east of Fort Charles.

When France declared war on Britain in 1778 and took neighboring British West Indies possessions, the military picture changed profoundly and it appeared only a matter of time before Barbados would be taken as well. England dispatched troops and naval forces to Barbados. By 1783, with the promise of more troops to come and the island unable to accommodate the great numbers already here, temporary barracks and facilities were built, but with the ending of the US Revolutionary War that same year the bulk of the British troops were withdrawn.

Modern-day Marines

To prevent any further threats to its West Indies territories, in 1785 the British Government decided to establish permanent land forces in the Windwards and Leewards with Barbados as headquarters. Construction of the British Garrison began in earnest in 1789 after the purchase of some 64 acres (26 hectares) of land. By the time construction of British facilities began, St Ann's Fort embraced some 14 acres (5.7 hectares), which were still under the domain of the Barbados Colony government. The first British buildings – the Powder Magazine and Ordnance Storehouse – were built inside St Ann's walls, along with the Drill Hall barracks on the north side of the fort, even though the British Army did not merge St Ann's into the Garrison until 1811. Fort Charles remained out of the loop until 1836. Various other buildings were constructed, including the Commissariat Provision Store in 1801, which today serves as the Light & Power Company building.

When troubles with France recurred in the late 1700s (at the time of the French Revolution), Barbados became the springboard for expeditions to nearby territories held by the enemy. Even though many Garrison buildings were up by this time, they proved woefully inadequate for the troop numbers moving through the island. This problem, compounded by further spats in the Napoleonic Wars in 1803, prompted swift construction of more facilities.

With each renewed threat, more buildings sprang up, and the area soon consumed more than 150 acres (61 hectares). Construction continued at a rapid clip, even though the role of the Garrison changed with the times. As the wars with France abated, internal problems erupted. The slave revolt of 1816 was put down by the British regiment, and this event led to the establishment of a chain of signal stations manned by the Royal Artillery.

The 1831 Great Hurricane, which nearly flattened the whole island, severely damaged much of the Garrison, with one account reporting, 'almost every building on the Garrison was demolished.' But it was yellow fever more than anything else that made life miserable for the troops, with many dying from the mosquito-borne disease each year. Troop numbers seemed to peak around 1815, with some 2,700 stationed at the Garrison. The last British troops left the Garrison in November 1905, and in January 1906, the 1st West India Regiment withdrew, leaving a small number of officers to tie up loose ends.

The Garrison functioned for 126 years as it was intended, leaving in its wake a legacy of buildings, artillery and artifacts that live on today.

Depending on the time of day you arrive, your first stop on a tour of the Garrison might be the Barbados Gallery of Art (*see page 32*) on the corner across from the children's play park. But since this tour makes a complete circle, you can also begin at the Main Guard and the cannon collection, as we do here. This is the best option if you arrive before the gallery opens at 10am.

The **National Cannon Collection** is unique since it represents the largest collection of 17th-century English iron guns in the world and is one of two collections that includes a gun with Cromwell's Republican Arms. After Cromwell died orders were given for all his possessions to be destroyed and the Barbados cannon with his crest is the only one known to be found on land – perhaps because the order never reached the holder, who may have been in St Lucy. The collection totals some 150 guns, about a dozen of which are posted in front of the Main Guard looking onto the Savannah. Others are posted at St Ann's Fort.

The clock tower

The **Main Guard**, built in 1804, is the centerpiece of the Garrison and houses two important features; the clock tower and the coat of arms. Court martials and other matters were handled here, and a small guard house at the back of the building held prisoners. Today the Main Guard houses the office of the Garrison Secretary and there are plans to open a Visitor Information Center here.

The **clock tower** is dated 1803 and was made by Dwerri and Cater of

Colonial style

London. The coat of arms on the front of the building, which Major Hartland recently discovered dates back to 1803 as well, is made of Coadestone – an artificial stone developed by Eleanor Coade around 1780. She died before revealing the formula for this durable clay substance, although efforts to discover the 'recipe' continue today. The coat of arms was painted white but the stone itself is actually tinged with pink. Another unusual feature of this coat of arms is that the animals are seen relaxing instead of in the rampant stance which is more common.

The **Drill Hall** has a long history of different uses, beginning in 1790 as a soldiers' barracks. In 1822 it became an armory and from 1881 until the British left it served as the Garrison headquarters. After 1905 possession passed to the Barbados Government, who used it for a gymnasium and drill hall for the Volunteers Force (hence the name). Around this time it was rented out for public events, becoming one of the island's favored dance venues in the 1970s. Today it is the Defense Force officers' and sergeants' mess hall. Queen Elizabeth II dined here during one of her visits to Barbados.

St Ann's Fort, also part of the Defense force compound, can be seen from the road. It's beveled stone walls form a hexagon enclosing 1½ acres (0.2 hectares). A look-out tower, built in the 1830s, served as part of the signal system and operated as a wireless station from 1914 to 1918, communicating with ships.

The **Naval Magazine**, extending under St Ann's Fort, is thought to have been built in the late 1700s. A tunnel leading out was probably used for the secret loading and unloading of arms.

Brigade House is now a clinic, but in 1819 it was the Brigade Major's quarters. After 1862 it became the chaplain's quarters.

Savannah Lodge, now occupied by the Caribbean Conservation Association and the Museum Association of the Caribbean, was originally a store and later converted into a private residence. In

1927, the government bought the property to house the Colonial Secretary and renamed it Savannah Lodge.

Letchworth, **Geneva** and **Rafeen** are now private residences, but were originally the Ordnance Hospital. Built before the Great Hurricane of 1831, the hospital survived, mainly due to its extensive ironwork. It is thought that the main hospital was Geneva. Its iron pillar supports also made it a good hurricane shelter. After 1855 it was converted into a recreation, library and theater facility.

The **Blocks 'A', 'B'** and **'C' Officers' Barracks** are now government offices. Blocks 'A' and 'B' were termed the 'New Barracks' in 1824, when they each housed 400 men. **Block 'C'** dates from 1807.

The **Barbados Museum** (Monday to Saturday 9am–5pm, Sunday 2–6pm) is a fascinating museum that is well worth visiting. Formerly the military prison, it was built between 1817 and 1818. In 1933 the government leased the complex to the budding Barbados Museum and Historical Society, which has remained here since. It is filled wall to wall with history, from its brickwork architecture to its many artifacts ranging from Amerindian relics to modern art. The **Cunard Gallery** holds West Indian paintings and prints dating back

Exhibit in the Barbados Museum

to the 1600s. The **Jubilee Gallery** is the focus of the island's social and cultural development and the **Temporary Exhibition Gallery** displays a wide range of visiting shows. The **library** contains a wealth of West Indian historical material from plantation records to maps and genealogical records. Youngsters are catered for in the interactive **Children's Gallery**.

According to extensive research in the early 1990s, **Bush Hill House** was discovered to be the true site of George Washington's accommodation when he visited Barbados in 1751. The current house is the oldest residence in the Garrison area, and existed from at least 1804. It was originally a two-story stone building, but has undergone many changes over the years.

In the Children's Gallery

The **water mill** and **bath house** near this complex entrance date from at least 1793, perhaps earlier. Outside the compound a monument commemorates 'the 14 soldiers and one married woman' killed in the Barracks and Hospital during the Great Hurricane.

The Officers' Quarters for the Royal Artillery and Royal Engineers included **Horseshoe Manor**, **The Bungalow** and **Caledon**, now the Barbados Gallery of Art (*see below*). The buildings have been too dramatically changed since their construction in 1824 to say much about their original design.

Stafford House was built in 1812 as a barracks for the Ordnance or Royal Artillery. The building later accommodated the military band and their instruments. The current facade masks the underlying brick and stone work.

The **Savannah**, now a racetrack, was originally a swamp which was used in dry periods for various purposes. After the discovery of the link between yellow fever and mosquitoes by the early 19th century, underground drainage trenches were put in to keep it perpetually free of water. The Savannah then became a year-round parade ground and sports arena. The first horse race was held here in 1840. Today the Garrison is a venue for all manner of sports and leisure activities hosting parades and ceremonies on occasions such as Independence Day (November 30). The grounds are managed by the Barbados Turf Club which operates three racing seasons per year: January to April; June to August and October to December. (For track information call the BTC, tel: 426-3980.)

Opened in October 1996, the **Barbados Gallery of Art** (Tuesday to Saturday 10am–5pm, closed Sunday and Monday) is a small non-profit fine arts museum with a national mission to collect, exhibit, research and preserve local and Caribbean art for the public. This is the island's sole art museum and one of only a few in the Eastern Caribbean. There are two galleries, each containing works from a wide range of artists. Gallery 1 showcases pieces from its growing permanent collection and Gallery 2 focuses on visiting shows by local artists and international traveling exhibitions and private collections. The galleries change their exhibits quarterly (tel: 228-0149 for current and up-coming exhibits).

Horsing around at the Savannah

After your tour have lunch in the **Museum Café** with its cobblestone courtyard, or try **Pegasus Restaurant** in the BTC Grand Stand (Monday to Friday noon–2.30pm and on race days). Alternatively, take the main road heading up the south coast to the Chattel Plaza which has a good sandwich shop (**The Lunch Club**) and wine bar (**39 Steps**). Opposite the Plaza is the **Kirby Gallery** (Monday to Friday, 10am–6pm, Saturday until 2pm), which has an excellent collection of art for sale.

A half-day option linking the principal attractions around Bridgetown. It includes the Malibu Visitors Centre, the Mount Gay Rum Visitor Centre (BNT), Medford Craft Village and the Tyrol Cot Heritage Village (BNT). *See map on pages 18–19*

—You may want to take advantage of the beach and lunch facilities at Malibu. If you do want to 'beach it' here, it's worth calling ahead. as they are occasionally booked out by cruise ships (tel: 425-9393)—

Get onto the ABC Highway and to the Warrens roundabout. Continue on to University Hill. At the roundabout at the bottom of the hill take the second exit to join Spring Garden Highway. Look for the Brighton exit – opposite the Workbench Factory – and turn right. When you come to the stop a few seconds later, turn right again and follow the road almost to its end. **Malibu Visitors Centre** (9am–5pm daily with tours every half hour) is on the left.

Of the many spirits tours Barbados has to offer, this is perhaps the most comprehensive; it combines a tour of the island's largest distillery and demonstrations of traditional barrel-making, with beach and watersports facilities. The center itself is unusually designed, with muted purples, greens and blues in a mosaic of arches and A-frame angles; the souvenir shop stocks specialty items, including products bearing the Malibu logo, attractive sea glass jewelry and other unusual local craft items.

The guided tour takes you into the distillery, where you can see the step-by-step fermenting, distilling, refining and aging process in action. Enthusiastic and well-informed guides reveal all kinds of fascinating information, including how by-products are used for everything from cures for arthritis to household cleansers. The tour continues to the barrel-making area where the 'coopers' reconstruct white oak whisky barrels for rum aging and storage. The coopers also make novelty items and furniture from the spent barrels.

The tour cost includes use of the center's lovely beach and lounge chairs, changing rooms, showers and lockers. There is also a bar and huge barbecue for lunches (11.30am –2.30pm), along with a watersports concession where you can rent gear. The center

Potent mix

Connoisseur at Mount Gay

offers a pass for visitors who want to spend the day.

If you also want to take in Mount Gay on your tour (*see below*), go back to Spring Garden Highway. Since there is no right turn, you have to travel back to Da Costa Mannings sign (at the Ham Center) and turn around. Drive the length of the highway towards town and look for the Mount Gay sign and a left turn called Exmouth.

Mount Gay (9am–4pm with tours every 45 minutes; BNT) is one of the world's oldest distilleries. The 30-minute tour includes a video presentation and a tour of the distillery, bottling plant and aging area. This is another informative tour rich in detailed history spanning three centuries. While all the guides are knowledgeable and amiable, perhaps the best-known is head barman Chester, who provides an animated sampling experience at the end of the tour.

On leaving Mount Gay turn left on to the Highway and take a right at the traffic lights if you would like to join or find out more about one of the exciting **Atlantis Sub** tours (tel: 436-8929; tours Tuesday to Saturday). Atlantis Submarines offer guests three ways to experience Barbados' underwater world: the Submarine and Seatrek (semi-submersible) tours are both 1½ hours long; snorkel tours run to at least two hours. To reach the Atlantis office continue to the

Mahogany furniture in the making at Medford Craft Village

roundabout and take the right-hand exit to the Shallow Draught; veer to the compound on your right, where you will see the imposing multi-decked *MV Harbour Master* at dock, loosely styled on a Mississippi steam-boat. **Harbour Master** (tel: 430-0900) have day and evening cruise packages.

Medford Craft Village (Monday to Friday 8am–5pm, Saturday 8.30am–1pm) is the island's hub for mahogany crafts. To reach it from Atlantis Sub return to the main intersection at the start of the Highway, this time continue straight on. In less than a mile you will see the small yellow sign (on the left) directing visitors to Medford Craft Village. Turn right and at the stop sign turn left into Baxter's Road; just a few yards ahead is Medford's yellow wall and entrance.

This is a real behind-the-scenes look at mahogany craft production. You can watch the artisans at work and browse for souvenirs and art treasures. The real treat is the main Medford shop, selling work rarely seen in the retail outlets around the island, including magnificent, highly polished coffee tables, and ornately carved chairs as well as beautiful abstract 'root art' and Medford's famous mahogany clock collection.

Coming out of Medford turn left to the **Tyrol Cot Heritage Village** (weekdays 9am–5pm; BNT) and through the bustling little suburb of Eagle Hall. Go straight through the traffic lights and follow the road to Codrington Hill. Tyrol Cot is on the left before the traffic lights.

One of the Barbados National Trust's heritage sites, Tyrol Cot was the home of the late Sir Grantley Adams, Barbados' first premier, and his wife Lady Adams from 1929 until her death in 1990, and it was here that they raised their one son, J.M.G.M. 'Tom' Adams, the island's second prime minister. The house was a hive of political activity from the 1930s to the 1960s, when Sir Grantley was fighting for the rights of the working class.

The house itself was built in 1854 by William Farnum, a prominent builder of the 19th century. It is an excellent example of that period's sturdy architecture, with its blend of modest Palladian, classical and tropical vernacular elements. The interior has high ceilings, arched doorways, classical jalousied windows and antique furniture owned by the Adams family, including a Victorian revolving bookcase, a Regency-style double-ended couch and many hand-crafted Barbadian mahogany pieces. The house is filled with memorabilia.

On the 3 acres (1.2 hectares) of landscaped grounds the Trust has developed a craft village using the chattel house blueprint for shops and studios, including silk-screening, leathercraft and basketry outlets. There is a Cockspur Rum shop and Sweetie Shop.

To head home, continue up the hill to the ABC Highway.

4. The West Coast

A leisurely trip up the island's west coast to Speightstown in St Peter. Visits to St James Parish Church, Folkestone Marine Park and the Sir Frank Hutson Sugar Museum (BNT) and Portvale Sugar Factory. With stops for swimming and shopping, you can make a whole day of this tour. *See map on pages 18–19.*

This is an easy drive in terms of directions as you stay on the same road for most of the trip, driving up Highway 1 to Speightstown. If you are staying on the west coast, you can join Highway 1 at whatever point is convenient.

From the south coast take the ABC Highway to the Warrens roundabout, continuing straight over to University Hill. As you descend the hill there is a lovely view of the harbor straight ahead. The clusters of white buildings you pass on the way are part of the University of the West Indies (UWI), which was established in 1948 and reached full university status in 1962. At the roundabout at the bottom of the hill, turn right and drive up the west coast.

Along the 5-mile (8-km) drive to Holetown are a number of windows to the sea. Tourist activity increases as you continue north reaching a bustling level at the bottom of Holders Hill, where there

Golf at Sandy Lane

are a number of quaint boutiques and antique shops. Along the way is **Bombas**, a delightful beach bar with an attractive vista of Paynes Bay.

An area of lush greenery where trees line the road is the approach to **Sandy Lane Hotel** and its affiliated estates. The hotel, which was reputed to be the best on the island, saw its heyday in the 1960s and '70s. Today the owners are implementing a controversial plan to rebuild the hotel. It is due to reopen in summer 2000. You will see the Golf Club entrance on the right; the course, which remains open, is also being dramatically extended to 45 holes. If you want to stop for a swim or a walk on the long, well-kept beach here, return to the public entrance at the south end of the hotel.

As you enter **Holetown** proper, you will notice the brightly painted **Chattel House Village** on the right. Opened in late 1996, the village is a cluster of chattel house-style shops fashioned after its sister St Lawrence Gap village. A browse through the village makes an enjoyable shopping expedition (the entrance is at the Royal Bank of Canada turn-off opposite the Chefette fast food outlet).

There are two major shopping malls in Holetown: **Sunset Crest Plazas** 1 and 2, which have lively shops including a supermarket,

A west coast way to start the day

duty-free outlets, local shops and eating places. On the other side of the road is a selection of beachside restaurants. Check out **Baku Beach** which has a pool and brasserie; **Cocomos**, with an appealing Caribbean ambiance, or the **Surfside** restaurant, tucked away behind the Parish Post Office and Police Station. If you just want a snack try **Patisserie Flindt** for its sumptuous pastries.

In front of the Police Station, the **Holetown Monument** commemorates the 1625 landing of the first English settlers. Erected in 1905, this monument bears the wrong date of the landing, an error that was eventually corrected with another plaque in 1975.

Coming out of Holetown on the left is **St James Church**, site of the island's first church. The original wooden church was replaced by a stone building in the late 1600s, but was destroyed in the 1780 hurricane; most of the present church dates from the 1800s. It contains many historic artifacts, including the baptismal font from 1684 and the original church bell, which pre-dates the United States Liberty Bell by more than 50 years.

Traveling north for about 1 mile (1.6km) out of Holetown you will come to the government-run **Folkestone Marine Park** (daily 9.30am–5pm). Folkestone has a good beach, many water-based facilities and activities, fresh-water showers and shops, as well as a small and fairly basic interpretive center and museum with marine and coastal environment displays, exhibits of the island's fishing industry and a salt water aquarium. The underwater park zone extends from Sandy Lane to Colony Club; here you can rent gear for snorkeling around the fringe reef, hire a boat for diving (ask to be taken to see the local turtles), or take a trip in a glass-

In the swing

bottom boat that plies the area. The park, like other favored dive and snorkel spots on the island, reveals a rich underwater world of living corals, small colorful fish, sea anemone and occasionally larger fish such as barracuda.

Less than 1 mile (1.6km) north of Folkestone you will come to the **Colony Club** beach entrance. In addition to being a lovely beach, this spot offers a peek at **Heron Bay House**, built in 1947 by the late Ronald Tree, a member of Winston Churchill's British parliament. This house, where he often wintered, enjoyed a steady stream of movie stars, heads of state and royalty, including Princess Margaret, Sir Winston and Lady Churchill, Sophia Loren, Ingrid

Bergman, Pierre Trudeau and Adlai Stevenson. Designed by English architect Sir Geoffrey Jellico, Heron Bay is a Palladian villa based on the Villa Maser design. Set in 20 acres (8 hectares) of magnificently landscaped grounds with huge gardens and wooded areas, the main coral stone wings form a semi-circle around the courtyard, where a massive chandelier hangs. The complex includes a number of other buildings, such as the pink house, with its octagonal windows. The National Trust Open Houses Program (every Wednesday from January to April) sometimes includes this property on its list.

We now travel past a stretch of other opulent properties and glorious homes that line the beach all along this coast to Speightstown. Among

Catching the sunset, Mullins Beach

them you will pass the **Lone Star Garage**, a beautiful beachside restaurant. Just after entering the parish of St Peter you will come to the spectacular **Mullins Beach** with its lively beachside bar.

From there, continue north and follow the signs for **Speightstown**. The narrow streets, the two-story balconied buildings and the little fishing boats that dot the beaches combine to make Speightstown special. Once a primary seaport of Barbados, it is one of the last 18th-century ports in the Caribbean region. It was known popularly as 'Little Bristol' for its trading links with Bristol in England, but named Speightstown after William Speight, who owned the land where the town now stands.

A good lunch stop in Speightstown is **Fisherman's Pub**, a bustling beachfront haunt that offers good local food, low prices and hearty helpings. Their specialty is steamed fish, served daily. After exploring Speightstown you can venture a bit further north or make your way back to Holetown. If you prefer to eat a light lunch here, stop at **Kitchen Korner** (2nd Street), a great gourmet sandwich shop.

Just after the bridge on the way into Holetown is a left turn on to Highway 1A, heading inland. Take this road to the roundabout and drive north on Highway 2A for less than 1 mile (1.6km) to reach the **Sir Frank Hutson Sugar Museum** and **Portvale Sugar Factory**

Sir Frank Hutson Museum

(Monday to Saturday 9am–5pm). The museum, in the old boiling house, is small but packed with interesting artifacts, equipment and photos depicting scenes from the early days of the sugar industry. Between January and May you can tour the working Portvale Factory and watch sugar manufacturing in action, from its genesis as cane to its crystalline conclusion. You can also learn about the rigorous production controls, and the steps to make such by-products as 'cane syrup' and molasses.

You can take one of two routes back to your base from here. Go back the way you came if you want to shop in Holetown or make a beach stop. To head directly home, stay on Highway 2A to the Warrens roundabout, and then back to the ABC Highway.

5. The Far North

This is a day tour of the spectacular north coast. It includes Harrison Point lighthouse, Animal Flower Cave, North Point and River Bay. It is recommended that you take a picnic, but failing that you can have a sandwich at the Animal Flower Cave. *See map on pages 18–19.*

St Lucy is often overlooked by visitors because it lacks the developed attractions of other parishes, but if you enjoy exploring areas slightly off the beaten track, this tour makes an excellent day out. Follow the west coast itinerary through Speightstown in St Peter. A good stop off for a snack and a swim along the way is Mullins Beach (*see page 38*), just before Speightstown.

Continue up the coast and pass through **Six Men's Bay**, a busy little fishing area with colorful boats lining the beachfront. The road soon cuts inland, linking up to Highway 1B going north. At this point the route runs through flat drab land and housing developments but once you reach the coast, you will see it was well worth the drive.

Six Men's Bay

A sign indicates a left turn for **Harrison Point Lighthouse**, one of three lighthouses on the island still in operation. Following this road, which narrows as you get closer to the lighthouse, you pass the Barbados Youth Service

Testing the water, Animal Flower Cave

headquarters, formerly a United States Naval base. From here the road turns into what is locally called a 'cart road' – a narrow dirt track. It is safe to drive through.

Today, the working lighthouses are maintained but unmanned. From the cliff you can see the start of the rugged north coast.

Come out from the lighthouse and continue north to your next stop, Animal Flower Cave (well sign-posted). The **Animal Flower Cave** (daily 9am–4pm) reached a low state of repair at one point, but it has been revived and now enjoys a steady stream of visitors.

This cave is the island's only accessible sea cave. It was discovered in 1780 by two English explorers. Its coral floor is estimated to be 400,000 to 500,000 years old and the 'younger' coral section above the floor about 126,000 years old. The dating was carried out by the German Geographical Institute, and visitors can see a 'map' of the dating work in the bar-restaurant. The cave now stands some 6ft (1.8 meters) above the high tide mark even though it was formed at sea level. This is because Barbados is rising by about 1 inch (2.5cm) per 1,000 years.

The managers, who also run the bar-restaurant Pirate's Tavern, have a well-trained and amiable group of guides to take visitors into the cave for a nominal fee. The first thing to notice is the huge coral steps leading down into the cave. Built around 1912, these steps are a remnant from the cave's days as a dancehall, when people from around the island arrived by horse and buggy for a weekend of seaside relaxation and fun.

Down in the cave guides will point out formations and sea anemones, locally called 'animal flowers,' as well as other artifacts from bygone days, including the braces in the coral ceiling where lanterns once hung. Several windows to the ocean offer good views. On calm days you can also go into a 'room' off to the right and swim in the natural pool, or at least take in yet another awesome view of the Atlantic through this larger sea window. Back up on land, the bar-restaurant serves drinks and hearty sandwiches. Its walls and ceiling are covered in business cards from around the world, and the staff will happily loan you the glue to add your own. This collection has been amassing since the early 1970s when the cave first opened to the public.

Outside the bar area are a few cannons from sunken ships. At one time they included one of the few known cannons to bear the crest of Oliver Cromwell (this particular cannon is now in the Garrison collection, *see page 29*).

From here continue to North Point Surf Resort, a glorious hotel of the 1960s that was abandoned in the 1970s and left to decay. Follow the signs just outside the cave exit, making your way east: signs are well posted all along the way. The sea's fury has carved a magnificent cove at **North Point**, which is well worth seeing. When you arrive, park in the car park (lock your car) and walk through the bar area, passing the now defunct pool. From the detail of the coral work and the remnants of the design, it is not hard to imagine that this was once a stellar hotel. After several false starts at trying to revive the hotel, it now seems doomed to destruction by the salty elements.

Walk through the back and across the clumpy grass towards the sea and a stone wall. Following the wall to the left you will come to steps leading down to the bay. This is not a swimming stop, as the currents here are extremely dangerous, so despite its inviting appearance do not be tempted to take a swim. However, this is one of the island's pristine panoramas. The sea's rhythmic drubbing of the landscape has a mesmerizing effect that, for all its roar, is tranquilizing.

Rugged North Point

From here continue eastward to River Bay. At the junction, turn left and descend to the car park, picnicking areas and amenities. While swimming in the mouth of the sea and beyond is discouraged, a little wade in the shallow 'river' inlet is harmless. Popular with locals, this is an ideal picnic spot with lovely shaded areas and picnic tables all along both sides of the river. Both kids and adults enjoy climbing around and exploring the area.

From here make your way back, cutting inland to pass through the rural north (you will see a left-hand turn soon after leaving River Bay: follow that all the way to the roundabout, on Highway 1C and Duncan O'Neal Highway, and return along Highway 2A, the road above the Highway 1 coast road). Alternatively, return the way you came, stopping for a little shopping en route.

View the wildlife

6. The Northeast

This is a full day of sights, including the Wildlife Reserve (BNT) and Grenade Hall Signal Station (BNT), Farley Hill Park and a tour of the 17th-century plantation house, St Nicholas Abbey (BNT). Visit Cherry Tree Hill for fabulous views and see Morgan Lewis Mill (BNT), the region's last intact windmill. *See map on pages 18–19.*

–If your hotel packs picnic lunches, or if you have facilities to prepare one yourself, I recommend you take a picnic on this tour, as Farley Hill is perfect for a relaxing lunch. If not, you can drive down to Speightstown between stops–

This is a long itinerary so start out early. Get on the ABC Highway and exit at the Warrens roundabout and go north onto Highway 2A. Travel all the way up to Mile And A Quarter junction in St Peter. Turn right here, travel about half a mile (0.8km) and then turn right onto the Charles Duncan O'Neal Highway. Follow the signs to the **Barbados Wildlife Reserve** and **Grenade Hall Signal Station** (both BNT) (daily 10am–5pm).

The admission fee covers both attractions. The 4-acre (1.6 hectare) Wildlife Reserve, opened in 1985, was initially a woodland sanctuary for the indigenous Barbados green monkey and a few other local and regional creatures such as tortoise, the tiny Brocket deer and birds, including brown pelicans and peacocks. Over the years stock

Grenade Hall woodland

has increased and the reserve is now home to an intriguing menagerie. Take your time going through the meandering mahogany lined paths, and move along quietly. If you breeze through too quickly or make too much noise you may miss seeing some of the more shy creatures.

The reserve has several animals native to the region including the agouti (a red-eared guinea pig-like creature), hares, which were once common in Barbados, the alligator-like Caiman from Guyana, porcupine and iguana. You may also see pink flamingos, maras (from Africa), wallaby, otters and snakes, and the reserve has an aviary of mostly macaws and cockatoos.

What makes this stop so much fun is that most of the area is open, so animals run about freely. You may be hard-pressed to see monkeys as they tend to roam to other areas; however, try a visit around feeding time (3pm) and you'll be sure to see them.

The snack bar and reception area are beautifully finished in a rustic design using sugar factory relics. The bricks forming the pathways are also from old sugar factories.

Just next door – on the same compound – is Grenade Hall forest area and signal station. A visit to the restored signal station gives an insight into how the military communicated in the 19th century. Six of these stations were constructed at vantage points around the island, and by using semaphore the military could communicate island-wide in a matter of minutes.

The station has a display of artifacts, both military and pre-Columbian, and an audio loop recounts the drama of the 1816 slave revolt and other episodes in the island's history when this communication network was used.

Behind the signal station a 3-mile (5-km) rambling coral pathway takes you through a thriving woodland forest. Amusing 'question & answer' signs posted along the way bring this eco-system to life and teaches one about tropical forests, folk medicine and conservation.

Across the road is **Farley Hill National Park** (daily 7am–6pm), an idyllic spot for a picnic lunch (entrance fee US $1.50 per car) with a stunning panorama. This was the site of the magnificent 19th-century 'great house' Farley Hill, considered the island's most stately mansion. In 1956 the house was the scene of several sequences in the movie, *Island in the Sun*, but soon after it was destroyed by fire. Its ruins make for an interesting backdrop to the 17 acres (7 hectares) of land. The government bought the property in 1965 and the following year Queen Elizabeth II officially opened Farley Hill as a park.

If you are not picnicking, return to Mile And A Quarter and head back into Speightstown for lunch. As on the West Coast tour,

Modern-day farm worker

Fisherman's Pub is a good option with relatively low prices, plenty of specials to choose from and a welcoming ambience.

When you've finished eating, either return to Mile And A Quarter, or if you are coming from Farley Hill, go back to the start of the Charles Duncan O'Neal Highway and turn right on to Highway 1. From here follow signposts to **St Nicholas Abbey** (BNT) (Monday to Friday 10am–3.30pm); the drive from Farley Hill is no more than 10–15 minutes. If you are interested in plantation history, it is worth trying to arrive for the 2.30pm showing of a short film of the working plantation made in 1934 (this is also shown at 11.30am).

Built between 1650 and 1660, St Nicholas Abbey is one of the few remaining Jacobean homes in the western hemisphere. The house is magnificently furnished much as it was 300 years ago. While many furnishings have come and gone with its various owners, several pieces date back to the 17th and 18th centuries. Of special note is the grandfather clock, which stands on the staircase. Made by J. Thwaites of London in 1759, it has occupied the same spot for more than 200 years.

A tour of the property includes most of the downstairs, the 'backyard' with its 'four-seater' outhouse and the original bath house equipped with tubs and an old-fashioned water heating apparatus. The tour includes a comprehensive explanation of most aspects of the house, its furnishings, plantation operations and ownership.

St Nicholas Abbey

The early history of St Nicholas Abbey's ownership is as colorful as the furnishings. Its original owner was Benjamin Beringer, but after scandals involving land squabbles, sexual affairs and a murder, John Yeamans emerged as the property's second owner. He was knighted, and soon after was appointed Governor of South Carolina, a post he took up in 1672.

The property passed through many hands, usually by inheritance, but in the early 1800s it was bought out of Chancery Court (debt). The current owner, Lieutenant Colonel Stephen Cave, is one of a long line of Caves through whose hands the property has since passed. Colonel Cave inherited the abbey in 1964 and lives here part time.

St Nicholas Abbey's 420 acres (170 hectares) of plantation land extends to **Cherry Tree Hill** (turn left as you leave the abbey). The road there leads through heavy canopies of trees then opens out to a lovely panorama of the East coast.

Continuing down this road brings you to **Morgan Lewis Mill** (BNT) (daily 9am–5pm), used for grinding cane in the 18th and 19th centuries. The only intact sugar windmill in the Caribbean, it is on the World Monuments Fund list of 100 Most Endangered Sites in the World. The Dutch influenced mill is a typical example of the island's two-century tradition of wind-powered cane grinding. It has undergone major restoration work and you can still see the fully intact wheel house and sails.

Driving back to your base, you can take one of two routes – either continue south a mile or so (about 1.5km) until you meet the Charles Duncan O'Neal Highway and take that back past Farley Hill and the Reserve to return the way you came, or if you feel adventurous and want to see another side of Barbados, continue past the highway and try your hand at wending through the maze of scenic but confusing roads that cut through the midst of the Scotland District to Highway 2A. Armed with your map, a fair sense of direction, humor and patience, you can amble through sleepy villages and pick your way back. Views on the way are magnificent, and you will see the real heart of the island.

At least three routes will lead you to Highway 2A. The best of these is Orange Hill via Gregg Farm. However, if you miss that one, there are other routes which also connect to 2A. Signs may help, but don't depend on them as many are in disrepair and unreadable. Private signs pointing out directions to various attractions may be more helpful for getting your bearings. The most important thing is to roll with it and work your way west to Highway 2A.

The slow way home

This is a full-day tour through the heart of Barbados with visits to three of the island's biggest attractions: Harrison's Cave (BNT), Welchman Hall Gully (BNT) and Flower Forest. On the return, it makes a shopping stop at Earthworks and The Potters House. *See Map on pages 18–19.*

—Because Harrison's Cave has some very busy periods when passengers from the cruise ships visit, it can be worth calling in advance to make a booking (tel: 438-6640); otherwise you may have to wait in line for a long time—

In Harrison's Cave

Make your way on to the ABC Highway and exit at the Jackson roundabout. After driving through the little village of Jackson, you will see the old **Sharon Moravian Church** on your left. The Moravians, who came to Barbados in 1765, were the first missionaries to educate the slaves and introduce them to Christianity. Sharon, built in 1799, was seriously damaged in the Great Hurricane of 1831, but rebuilt in 1834.

Continue on this road for a few miles and follow signs to **Harrison's Cave** (daily 9am–4.30pm). Filled with streams, cascading water, pools and stalactites and stalagmites, this is one of the finest natural caverns in the region. While historical records of the cave date back to 1796, it remained unexplored until 1970. After considerable development, the cave was opened to the public in 1981 and has become one of the island's top attractions. Tours are conducted by trams, which travel down into the cave every half hour. A slide presentation is shown before the tour and there is a short but colorful nature walk which you can take before or after your tour, plus a Visitor Center, refreshment stand and handicraft shop.

Next on this itinerary is the Flower Forest. Leaving Harrison's Cave, continue north (right) to the Bloomsbury junction with the little 'bamboo village' (industrious locals have converted this area into a bustling handicraft center that has become a stopping point for cruise ship passengers and other island tours). Make a right here; just ahead the bridge wall on your left offers a stunning view of the eastern coast. You may want to stop here and examine the wares of the local hawkers.

Continue on this twisting road, passing a large dairy farm on the way. You will see signs indicating when to turn left for the

Down a leafy lane in the Flower Forest

Flower Forest (daily 9am–5pm). Described as a cross between a botanical garden and a nature trail, this is a 50-acre (20-hectare) explosion of greenery with commanding vistas of the island's Scotland District. You can take from an hour to a day to stroll along the wending paths and see a virtual wonderland of tropical plants, from gorgeous blooms to magnificent trees. Afterwards have a light lunch and browse in the gift shop in the main lobby.

After the Flower Forest, make your way back to the 'bamboo village,' this time turning right to carry on to Welchman Hall Gully, which is around the corner from Harrison's Cave. Owned and operated by the Barbados National Trust, **Welchman Hall Gully** (daily 9am–5pm) is about a 1-mile (1.6-km) hike through a deep, densely wooded gully filled with a tremendous variety of trees, plants and flowers. It formed part of the network of caves linked to Harrison's until its roof collapsed to form a gully, and this is why it is so much deeper than the hundreds of other gullies that ribbon the island. It has been tended since 1860 when the then owners introduced a variety of exotic plants and blooms to its already rich vegetation. Later, the gully fell into neglect until it was adopted by the Trust in 1962, becoming the first organized natural site in Barbados.

Today the gully is rich in every shade of green imaginable. You will encounter large, impressive stands of bamboo, splashes of colorful flowers and massive decorative and fruit-bearing trees. As you reach the end of the trail, the scent of nutmeg may waft past, and on the ground you may see the web-like pieces of mace that cover the nutmeg.

The trail is well-marked and with the brochure to guide you, it is easy to identify the many trees and blooms. The silence is broken only occasionally by squawking birds or monkeys crashing around in the trees above.

Welchman Hall Gully

Explore with Highland Tours

Leaving Welchman Hall, turn left for the brief drive to **Highland Outdoor Tours**, where you can stop for refreshments, enjoy the stunning view and enquire about joining an organized tour at a later date. Highland Outdoor Tours is perched between the island's highest points and a real adventure through some 1,500 acres (610 hectares) of previously inaccessible lands, much of it privately owned. Guides lead excursions through four parishes, delivering one exciting panorama after another. The tours vary in length – from two hours to a whole day – and mode. You can walk, travel on horseback, or even ride a jitney. The day-long tour is a 5-mile (8-km) hike to the east coast, culminating in a well earned hearty Carib-style lunch (tel: 438-8069 for details of tours).

I recommend an adventurous route home, again through the heartland area but taking in a few additional attractions. Turn right out of Highland Tours and just a mile (1.6km) or so ahead you will come to the Challenor School for the mentally handicapped on your left. Here make a right turn to take you around the second highest point on the island, **Mount Misery**. This meandering road will ultimately lead you on to Highway D, a well-paved, wide road. Turn left and follow the road past the old Vaucluse factory and on to Shop Hill, following signs for a left-hand turn to **Earthworks Pottery** (Monday to Friday 9am–5pm, Saturday 9am–1pm).

Master potter Goldie Spieler has carved a special niche for herself in this eyrie. You can buy beautiful functional art works from her own studio, which she operates with her son David, and also from the **Potter's House**, which has a veritable treasure trove of works by local artists and potters. The Spielers are famous for their hand-finished and decorated tableware with a distinctive Caribbean flavor. They throw virtually everything for the table, from huge serving pieces to spoon rests. Also on the site is an excellent small café with a great view.

To make your way home, follow the road down the hill to the junction by Sharon Moravian Church. Turn right here to go back to the Jackson roundabout and home.

A full day exploring the east coast. Drive up the East Coast Road and into Scotland District's picturesque Chalky Mount and the potteries. Visit **John C. Mayers Batik Gallery**, go down to the famous 'soup bowl' and Bathsheba, and lunch at the Atlantis Hotel with its fabulous overlook. Afterwards visit Andromeda Botanic Gardens (BNT). *See map on pages 18–19.*

–If you do this tour on a Sunday, the Atlantis has one of the best buffet lunches on the island–

To reach the east coast, take the ABC highway to the Lower Estate exit. This is not a roundabout, but a turn-off located between the Hothersal and Norman Niles roundabouts. Drive the few miles to the stop sign, then turn right onto what is Highway 3, though no signs tell you that.

The 30-minute drive to the east is both scenic and varied. Along the way you will see wavy lines of chattel houses among the cane fields and pass through backwater villages where time seems to stand still.

Half way along, just after **Market Hill** village, with its gas station and few stores, you will come to a three-way junction where a sign, half-buried under the canes, directs you left to the east coast. Soon after this you will pass **Andrew's Sugar Factory** where, depending on the time of year, you may see the great steam generators in action, breathing life into the cane grinding process. If it is cane grinding time (February through May), drive with extra care because the cane trucks are large, cumbersome and very slow.

At Parris Hill the road curves right and the coral walls are covered in community art. Continue on, passing the Grantley Adams School and the police station. From here it is literally all down hill. As you descend Horse Hill you will get your first view of the rugged east coast. This 10–15 minute drive is punctuated with glimpses of what's to come.

Eventually you will come to an intersection. The roads here, in any direction, are worth exploring. However, we will go left and start our tour with a drive down to 'Cattle Wash' and the East Coast Road. This passes along a beautiful stretch of the Atlantic coast. Drive past **Barclays Park**, a popular picnic area, and on to the Belleplaine junction.

At the Belleplaine Potteries shop make a sharp left and follow the road past the gas station and the Government Agricultural Station. About

a half mile (0.8km) further on a sign points left to Chalky Mount. Turn here, passing the Chalky Mount School and make your way up Coggins Hill. At the crest, a sign directs you left to the Potteries. (You will also see a sign directing you right: this is to a private potter's residence, which you can pass by on your way out.)

The potteries is less than half a mile (0.8km) further on, but before stopping there follow the road to the end for a short hike to the top of Chalky Mount for the view. (Park out of the way as buses use this open area to turn around.)

Chalky Mount juts up from the coast to about 550ft (168 meters) above sea level and offers one of the finest views on the island. At the road's end a path leads to the top of the Mount.

Coming back out, stop off at the Potteries. While this entire village was once bustling with potters working from their homes, only two potters work like this today. Yet the art is not dead, it has simply been centralized and most of the potters now work in the **Potteries** (Monday to Friday 8am–5pm; weekends 8am–3pm).

Chalky Mount house

The potters here will gladly show you how they work, and may even demonstrate the old manual 'kick wheel' on display, a 300-year-old pot-shaping method used until recently.

There is a nice range of work for sale, many pieces in muted tones. You can find decorative items as well as traditional pottery, such as 'monkey pots' and coal pots, which are both functional and good souvenirs. There is a wide selection of vases, plates, mugs, pitchers, candle shades and other items, including miniature pottery chattel houses.

On the way back from the Potteries, just before turning back onto East Coast Road, stop off at **Belleplaine Pottery**, an interesting co-op shop open seven days a week. The owner has a small bar and sells work by potters in the area. He also has a little garden with animals in the back.

Back on the East Coast Road, stop off at will for views (but not for sea bathing – the undercurrents here are deadly and you will most likely see the lifeguard stations empty). Climbing the hill again, this time go straight up, past the shop, and just as you come to the second shop turn left onto Cleavers Hill. Coming down you will see the batik signs directing you to **John C. Mayers Batik**.

John works from his home and while his opening hours are loosely 7.30am–4.30pm he is there most of the time and will also show visitors round on weekends. His folklore batiks have been exhibited locally and overseas. If you are following this itinerary on a

Bathsheba coast

weekend and want to make sure you catch him you can call ahead (tel: 433-9668).

Continue down the hill and just before the bottom turn left along a small road. Follow this for just a few minutes to enter the famous 'soup bowl' area popular with surfers. There is a small parking area, and you can take a stroll if you like.

A little further along the road are two pleasing refreshment stops: **Round House**, which was originally an elegant 19th-century home, has good food with a dash of local flair (it can be very busy at lunchtimes); and the antiquated **Edgewater Hotel** with its 'olde-worlde' charm – both have breathtaking views of the rocky coastline.

Travel back past the soup-bowl using the same route but this time veer left into **Bathsheba** proper. You will pass the popular **Bonito Bar** whose upstairs seating offers a good view of the surfing action. From here make your way up the hill (park at the bottom and walk if you feel like it), passing the Community Center with its mural depicting famous Barbadians.

Just past the Center is a left turn for the **Atlantis Hotel**, the best lunch stop on the coast (daily 11.30am–3pm). Perching on a ledge above the sea, the Atlantis is more than 100 years old, and its current owner, Mrs Enid Maxwell, has been running it since 1945. Secure a table on its balcony and watch the waves and the fishing activity while you eat. On Sundays, the hotel serves a buffet lunch, a fabulous spread of Bajan foods for under US$20; the rest of the week it offers an excellent full Bajan 'plate' lunch with choice of fish or chicken for around US$15.

Bearded Fig in Andromeda

Coming out of the Atlantis, continue up the hill to **Andromeda Botanic Gardens**, run by the Barbados National Trust (daily 9am–5pm). Nestled on a cliff overlooking the east coast, Andromeda's 6 acres (2.4 hectares) of blooms and shrubs represent one of the finest collections in the region. Andromeda was developed in 1954 by the late horticulturist Iris Bannochie as her weekend retreat. Eventually she opened it to the public and as she developed the gardens and acquired specimens from around the world, they became a major attraction. In 1988 she bequeathed the property to the people of Barbados.

The property is tastefully landscaped with ponds, streams, shady nooks, rocky ledges

and marvelous splashes of color. The orchid collection is vast and because of the tremendous variety there is almost always something in bloom. Andromeda also has one of the most extensive hibiscus and other flowering shrub collections in the Caribbean and the succulents are virtually a garden in themselves. Visitors are given guide sheets to enable them to identify the various flora.

To make your way home, continue up the hill, turn right and travel back the way you came.

9. Lower Central: St George Valley and St John

A day tour through the lower central region of St George Valley and St John where acres of rippling cane arrows are punctuated by quaint chattel houses. Visit historic sites including St George's Parish Church, Gun Hill Signal Station (BNT), Orchid World and St John's Parish Church (BNT). Stop off at Codrington College (BNT) for a walk along College nature trail, then to Bath, St John, on the Atlantic coast for a swim and a bite to eat. *See map on pages 18–19.*

Take the ABC Highway to the Norman Niles roundabout (between Hothersal and 'Bussa') and follow the road briefly for the Salters turn-off on the left – you will see the sign and a sign for Gun Hill. Stay on this road until you meet a four-way junction (Charles Rowe Bridge) with a gas station, then turn right. In a few hundred yards we come to **St George's Parish Church**, the island's oldest parish church. Destroyed in the 1780 hurricane and rebuilt in 1784 (it survived the 1831 Great Hurricane), St George's is a blend of Georgian and Gothic styles. It has the distinction of housing the spectacular Benjamin West painting of the Resurrection (over the altar).

The Lion at Gun Hill

Continuing on the same road, you will soon come to **Gun Hill Signal Station** (BNT), known affectionately as 'the Lion at Gun Hill' (Monday to Saturday 9am–5pm). Situated on the Gun Hill cliff at about 700ft (213 meters) above sea level, this signal station was restored by the Barbados National Trust in 1983 and is one of its prime heritage attractions.

Built in 1818, Gun Hill served not only as a signal station, communicating with the Christ Church and St Joseph stations, but also as a convalescence facility for soldiers

and their families, for the strong winds that sweep through this area kept it free of the dreaded yellow fever-carrying mosquitoes.

The site's landscaped gardens and the sweeping south coast panorama make this a favorite stop for visitors. And so it was almost 150 years ago, when the historian Schomburgk wrote in his *History of Barbados*, '...no stranger who visits Barbados should omit to see this spot.'

The landmark coral stone lion, carved in 1868 by Captain Henry Wilkinson with the assistance of four military laborers, stands 7ft (2 meters) tall. The Latin inscription at the base comes from Psalm 72, Verse 8: 'He shall have dominion also from sea to sea and from river unto the end of the earth' (referring, it is thought, to British dominion over the island).

'Road tennis' in St George

Continuing on Highway 3B you pass through one of the lushest districts on the island, and depending on the time of year you will see cane growing or being harvested. If you have an interest in horticulture, stop at Orchid World (look for the white walls and sign on your left). **Orchid World** (daily 9am–5pm) is one of the island's popular attractions; though still in its infancy, it houses an extensive collection of tropical orchids. When the gardens eventually reach maturity the collection is likely to surpass any outside of Singapore. Remain on this road, driving straight through Four Roads (past the fire station) and keep going. You will soon see **St John's Parish Church** straight ahead of you.

The church only dates back to 1836 – previous churches on the site were destroyed by hurricanes – but its centuries-old churchyard and surroundings are a treat for history buffs and even the mildly curious. Old tombstones with bizarre inscriptions populate this graveyard. The most notable belongs to Ferdinando Paleologus, buried here in 1670, a descendant of the brother of the last Byzantine Emperor, Constantine the Great. He fought as a Royalist in the English Civil War and after 1645 came as a refugee to Barbados where his family owned land. He served as St John's churchwarden for several years.

The church itself is a well-appointed, solidly-built Gothic-style structure. Its magnificent interior includes a beautifully crafted spiraling staircase and pulpit, carved from six different woods. The church also has a beautiful sculpture carved by Sir Richard Westmacott, sculptor of the Lord Nelson statue that stood for years in the center of Bridgetown.

Even the view from the churchyard is lovely, capturing a sweeping east coast panorama from a 800-ft (244-meter) escarpment. There is also a small drinks and souvenir shop on the property.

Coming out of St John's, turn left for Codrington College. Just past St John primary school turn left again and drive down the hill (Coach Hill), a steep, winding descent that provides tantaliz-

ing glimpses of the pristine coast. When you reach the bottom (Sergeant Street), continue on to the right and **Codrington College** (daily 10am–4pm, admission charge nominal) is only a few minutes' drive from here on the left-hand side. Tall cabbage palms line the lane through the entrance; you will see the lily pond on your left and the college directly in front of you.

The college was founded by Christopher Codrington, a visionary and benefactor of the poor in Barbados, who was born on the estate in 1668 and died in the original mansion in 1710, now the Principal's Lodge. Though a sugar planter by profession, his views and philosophy were very different from those of the other plantation owners of the day. In his will he stipulated that

Codrington's lily pond

his estate of 800 acres (323 hectares) be overseen by the Anglican missionary organization the Society for the Propagation of the Gospel, in order to establish a facility of divinity and general education for the children of slaves – a revolutionary idea at that time.

In fact the bequest was never followed according to Codrington's wishes, but instead educated wealthier boys to prepare them for Codrington (Theology) College.

The college buildings were constructed in 1743 and opened as Codrington Grammar School in 1745. It became a university level institution in 1830 and in 1875 gained its affiliation to the University of Durham, England, offering degrees from that institution. Since 1965 Codrington College has been part of the University of the West Indies and is the theological college of the Anglican Church for the West Indies Province.

The path to inner tranquillity and peace is reflected in the grounds and buildings of this institution, from the wonderful views and the serenity of the lily pond to the architecture of the college and the artifacts it holds. The college chapel is especially beautiful, with its glass mosaic of the Good Shepherd above an altar made of several woods, including ebony.

The college's nature trail, which is well marked, is a pleasant walk (short and on the flat) that begins by the lily pond and leads through the bamboo stand and into a wooded area. The flora is numbered and identified in the college brochure.

To continue to Bath, go back toward Coach Hill, then turn right down the hill just past where the road heads back up Coach Hill.

A few hundred yards ahead are the remnants of an old sugar factory. Turn right here and follow the road on to **Bath**. There is a large car park, toilet facilities, a snack bar and a beach with a lifeguard. This is generally a safe place to have a swim, but as a precaution ask first and stay to the left where the bottom is sandier.

There are picnic tables nestled under shade trees, and if you feel like another short walk you can follow the car park to its end where a dirt road leads to more beach houses. Follow this lane and turn uphill on the path just after the bridge where there is a small waterfall. You can continue turning uphill or keep straight along. The little path meanders along the coastline as far as Martin's Bay.

If you prefer a 'rum shop' snack, when you come out of Bath there are a couple of places at the base of Coach Hill on Sergeant Street where you can get fresh baked breads and sandwich fillers. Heading home you can go back the way you came or opt for the adventurous route, taking Highway 4.

In taking the latter route, you can make one last stop for a breathtaking view of the entire southeast coastline. Leaving Bath, turn left by the old smoke stack and go back towards Codrington College. Turn right immediately after the college and go up Society Hill. Turn right at the top and drive through Codrington High School's grounds and park by the Holy Cross church. Here you will get a special view of the southeastern end of the island as well as a closer look at a local private school, which has one of the nicest locations on the island.

To get on Highway 4 come back to the road and continue on to the junction (Society Plantation). Turn left and follow the road to the junction (at the gas station). Turn right and you are on Highway 4. While this route twists a bit at first, once on the highway, it is a pastoral drive which leads you back to your starting point.

Bath Beach

10. The Southeast

This full day includes visits to **Sunbury Great House** and the **Rum Factory and Heritage Park at Foursquare**, before making a beach stop at the little known **Harrismith Beach** and venturing on to view **Ragged Point Lighthouse**. Return via two of the island's most historic hotels: **Sam Lord's Castle**, a magnificent edifice and **The Crane Beach Hotel** with its stunning view.

–Although there are a number of refreshment options on this route, a packed lunch in one of the picturesque coves is particularly pleasant–

The first stop is Sunbury Great House (daily 9am–5pm). To get there join the ABC Highway and travel to the Emancipation Statue roundabout. Take the Mapp Hill exit (Highway 5) to the east. After about a 10-minute drive the road forks – veer left and enjoy this lengthy drive through the lush fields of St George. Ten more minutes along the road look out for the sign for Sunbury and a left turn (just before Six Cross Roads). The entrance to the property is on your left.

Sunbury Great House dates back to the 1660s. The entire house is open for viewing, each room impeccably furnished and decorated according to the period. This is a true plantation house tour that gives a very real sense of the lifestyle and living standards of the elite planter class in those early days. There is an extensive collection of old prints, china, glassware and antiques, as well as the region's largest assortment of horse-drawn carriages. You can roam into the gardens and surrounding wooded area and stop for a snack in the courtyard café.

Typical planter's drawing room

From Sunbury return along the same road, this time continuing straight on across the intersection with Highway 5. At the next junction turn right and you will see the entrance to the Rum Factory and Heritage Park shortly on your left.

The **Rum Factory and Heritage Park** at Foursquare (Monday to Friday 9am–5pm) opened in November 1996, the brainchild of well known local businessman and rum producer David Seale. A well-planned 9-acre (3.6 hectare) site encompassing culture, art, shopping, history and rum production, it offers several hours entertainment. The entry fee allows visitors the complete run of the park and factory.

On the complex you will find **The Art Foundry**, a gallery housed in a beautiful 250-year old building, where you can see permanent and visiting art displays. There are also six shops, a Folk Museum

Turning to pastures new

depicting traditional life in the 1950s and '60s, a full bar and snackbar available for refreshment. The Cane Pit Amphitheater puts on shows, concerts and other events (call ahead for a schedule: tel: 420-1977).

The property, which dates back some 350 years, was originally a working plantation, then a sugar factory was erected around 1730, later becoming Foursquare Sugar Factory, which operated until 1988. Remnants of the factory and its machinery pepper the complex, in the form of creative furniture in the Art Foundry and more formal displays in the outdoor sugar factory museum. Here the owners have recreated the story of sugar amid shady trees and a children's play area.

Factory relics can also be seen on the tour of what is the region's newest and most energy-efficient rum distillery. This computerized state-of-the-art distillery is the most modern in the world. As you follow the distilling process you will come to a 'fire wall', a remnant of the original factory, where you can glimpse a slice of sugar making 300 years ago.

For a swim at the delightful **Harrismith beach**, turn right at the main gate of the park and drive to Six Cross Roads (actually a roundabout) along Highway 6. Take the fourth exit passing Chefette (a popular local fast-food restaurant specializing in fried chicken) to your right. Follow this road for several minutes. Shortly after the sign for Mike's Trading on your right you will come to a sharp S-bend. Go down the secondary road instead of finishing the bend. Stay on this road to its end, then descend to the magnificent beach on foot. It is a long walk to this isolated, idyllic cove, so be prepared.

Sam Lord's Castle

This coastline has some of the most attractive bays on the island. Back on the road and on the way to **Ragged Point Lighthouse**, you may want to sample Bottom Bay, a little further up the coast from Harrismith, just look for the signpost. Continuing on the main road passing several villages until you

Beach at Sam Lord's

can see the lighthouse in the distance. Turn right at the Marley Vale sign and you will come to the lighthouse road ahead; you can drive right up to the building. This picturesque spot is worth exploring. Walk around the lighthouse and the ruins and follow the footpath to the cliff for awe-inspiring views on both sides.

The next stop is Sam Lord's. Return on the same road driving through the S-bend and taking a left hand turn at the sign for Mike's Trading. At the next junction take the left turn which leads straight to the main entrance of **Sam Lord's Castle** (open daily; tel: 423-7350), and below it the white sand of **Long Bay**. At the gate veer to the right for parking.

Sam Lord's was built in the 1820s by the infamous Samuel Hall Lord, a purported pirate and generally nefarious character. He was said to trick passing ships on to the surrounding reefs in order to plunder them. It is one of the finest edifices on the island. Standing on 72 acres (29 hectares) of land, the castle is now the centerpiece of an all-inclusive hotel resort. Visitors can view the ground floor of the Castle, gardens and shops which are open to the public. Lunch packages are also available, but they are pricey. If you fancy something lighter and less expensive try the **Pot & Barrel** outside the main entrance.

Standing with its four corners in line with the four points of the compass, this aptly named 'castle' is another example of the extravagant excesses of its period. The collection of art, furniture and china is impressive, and the walls are lined with huge portraits and paintings, primarily by leading European artists from the 17th and 18th centuries. The furniture, most of which Sam Lord imported from England, is Georgian or Sheraton-style mahogany.

Elaborate crystal chandeliers and plaster centerpieces decorate the ceilings. British architect Charles Rutter, who once worked on Windsor Castle, was responsible for much of the interior woodwork and plasterwork. With the help of two Italians, it took him almost four years to complete this detailed work. The surrounding grounds are filled with a variety of decorative and fruit trees, shrubs and flowering plants.

Continuing to **Crane Beach Hotel**, drive along the straight from Sam Lord's to the main junction and turn left. Follow this road around a sharp right bend, passing the Crane Beach sign, and go on several minutes more to the Hotel main entrance on your left.

This lovely old hotel was a plantation house in the mid-1700s. The main mansion, **Marine Villa**, which stands almost in its original form as part of the hotel's east block, is thought to have been built around 1790, possibly by Sam Lord before he built his castle. The building was converted into a hotel in 1887 and is one of the oldest on Barbados. In fact, one of its first famous guests in the 1890s was American cowboy 'Wild Bill' Hickock. Its romantic setting, perched on the cliff overlooking the turbulent Atlantic has made it a haven for honeymooners. The 40 acres (16 hectares) of land have a number of ruins at the south end and a dense coconut grove on the north side behind the beach. The hotel's landscaped gardens feature magnificent bronze sculptures by Enzo Plazzotta and a Roman

Crane Beach Hotel

pool. There is a visitor's entry fee, which is fully redeemable at the bar. (Pool packages are available for adults; only part of the fee is redeemable.)

The Crane's wide beach of fine powdery sand is one of the island's finest, and it enjoys the benefit of a protective reef that keeps turbulent undertows at bay. The front coral stone steps leading down to the beach are no longer in use but they are said to have been hand-carved in the 1700s. Just south of the property is the 'Horse', a secret bathing spot for women in the 1700s. The steps, cut out of the cliffs, are still there though the pool, which is wedged between the coral ledges, is not as placid as it was then.

If you wish to eat here while taking in the view there is an à la carte lunch menu (daily 12.30pm–3pm; service is typically slow) and live music. On Sunday there is a buffet of local fare.

To head home, turn left at the main entrance and keep following the windy course of this road past St Martin's church. After the sharp right bend by a stand of mahogany trees, veer left at the junction and continue on past the airport, joining the Highway at the second roundabout (right exit).

Continue on the Highway directly home or if you fancy a little recreational activity you can take the turn off at the first (Chickmont) roundabout and head to the **Barbados Academy of Golf**, at Balls

Taking the plunge

Complex (daily 8am–11pm; tel: 428-0119). Try a game of mini-golf or perhaps hit some balls at the island's only driving range. There is a small bar for refreshment at this wonderfully airy spot.

11. The South Coast

This is a straightforward coastal drive from Hastings to Silver Sands. The south coast is a hub of commercial activity and nightlife so you may want to visit the St Lawrence area, on another occasion, in the evening. There are lots of shopping opportunities, restaurants and beach stops.

West coast visitors should take the ABC Highway through the Pine where you will see the CBC satellite dish on the left after the first set of stop lights. Follow the road to the next lights, and on your left you will see the Barbados External Telecommunications (BET) office. Continue to the third set of traffic lights and turn left. Get in the right lane to exit on the far right at the next roundabout to the start of Rendezvous Hill. When you reach the bottom of the hill, turn right at the stop lights to reach Highway 7. For those of you staying on the south coast, join this tour at your leisure.

This route involves doubling back, so if you see something that grabs your interest you can have a closer look on your way back. The first stop is **Bertalan's Gallery** (by appointment only; tel: 427-0714) in **Hastings**. As you reach Regency Cove Hotel turn right on Queen's Way Road; Bertalan's Gallery sign is on the left. This gallery and foundry is the home of an ingenious local sculptor who fashions remarkable metal sculptures. Bertalan is an elderly man and although he produces little these days due to his advancing years his work remains unparalleled.

The sculptures are made first in wax and then covered with a plaster of Paris mold. The wax is melted out in an oven and the empty mold is then filled with molten metal. This 'lost wax' foundry technique is an ancient art form dating back some 3,000 years.

From here work your way back towards Rendezvous. The length of this coast is packed with banks, shopping plazas and eateries. Among the more interesting plazas is **Quayside**, on the left opposite Accra Beach Hotel. There is an excellent outdoor café, **The Fish Hook**, which sells grilled fish. Alternatively, grab a cappuccino or one of the other great drinks from **The Coffee Hut**. For souvenirs there is **Best of Barbados**, with many items featuring the work of local artist Jill Walker, or **The Yard**, which has mostly Caribbean crafts.

Across the road at **Accra Beach** you can usually find a coconut vendor. It is remarkable and sometimes alarming to watch how

Bertalan's Gallery

swiftly the coconuts are sliced open with a sharp machete. Try some coconut water straight from the coconut. As the coconuts mature the water or milk forms a jelly which is delicious. In very mature nuts there is no liquid just a hard white lining of the more commonly recognizable form of coconut.

Accra Beach is extremely popular with visitors and locals thanks to its convenient location, parking facilities and gentle surf. Here you will find a number of vendors selling beachwear and jewelry. If you are interested in buying, do not feel shy to barter. The frequency with which you will be approached can quickly become annoying. If you are not interested be polite but very firm.

Continue on Highway 7, passing Rendezvous. Take the third right turn after **Sandy Beach Hotel** by the Chinese restaurant. This tiny avenue will lead you to a glorious stretch of sand known as **Sandy Beach**. There is a natural lagoon here that provides particularly safe bathing for children and the protective reef can be explored at low tide. The strong breeze here, not typical of west coast beaches, makes sunbathing very pleasant; chairs can be rented for the day. If you are hungry sample the good value fare at the relaxed **Carib Beach Bar**; they have showers and live entertainment.

On leaving the Carib, turn right on to the main road and almost immediately on your left you will see the entrance to the **Graeme Hall Bird Sanctuary** on the island's last remaining coastal wetland and mangrove. It is a natural roosting and breeding ground for migratory birds, most notably egrets. With plans to preserve and nurture the area coming to fruition, Graeme Hall is set to become a distinguished birdwatching site.

If you don't wish to stop, continue on and take your next right turn into **St Lawrence Gap**. This one-way strip is the hub of the south coast action and full of hotels, eating places and shops. Our stop is the **Chattel House Village**, well into the Gap on the left, a cluster of chattel house-style shops with local arts, crafts and souvenirs. These shops are similar in design, but not in content, to the Holetown chattel village. Also worth a stop is a shop called **The Monkey Pot** which appears soon after you enter the Gap and further along the road is **Caribbean Walkers World**. If you are ready for lunch, a good choice is **B4 Blues** open noon–5pm Monday–Friday (*see Eating Out, page 76 for details*).

Follow St Lawrence Gap to its end, passing Dover Convention Center and various hotels until you reach Highway 7, where you need to turn right.

Next stop is **Oistins**, where you can visit the fish market on the right in the center of town. If you have cooking facilities in your accommodation, you might want to buy some 'boned' flying fish. Barbadians have made quite a skill of filleting this slender fish, transforming it into a staple dish. They are quick and easy to steam or grill, but are most typically eaten fried. The fish market is a hive of activity in season with a bevy of 'boners,' hawkers and 'cleaners' all busily working. On weekends – particularly Friday nights when there is the **Oistins Fish Fry** – the market area is packed until late with party goers and revelers and music blares out of every rum shop and stall.

On Rockley Beach

Oistins is primarily a fishing town and while there is little else of interest here, the small fishing boats and market make it well worth seeing. From here continue south and just outside Oistins veer right at a fork, minding the oncoming traffic. Follow this road a few hundred yards to a T-junction, where you turn left. (If you choose to turn right instead you will come to **Miami Beach/Enterprise Beach**, which is a peaceful, scenic beach stop.)

After that, simply follow the road or take the right turn that loops into the fancy Atlantic Shores residential area. You will be able to spot the **South Point Lighthouse** in the center of the housing area. Because of the extensive development, driving through this area can be confusing. Follow the road inland, through twists and turns until a church with a green roof appears on the right. Turn left, down the hill into **Silver Sands**. Keep loosely to the coast, taking the first left turn and following the signs to Silver Rock, our lunch stop.

Silver Rock offers inexpensive, hearty local fare in a laid-back gazebo-style beach restaurant where you can watch the windsurfers in the waves. Top international professional and amateur windsurfers come to practice here, many staying the whole season from January to May. International windsurfing competitions are held here in January.

If you are inclined to do some windsurfing yourself, Silver Rock Windsurf Shop is just next door to the restaurant. Owned and operated by renowned windsurfer Brian Talma, this is a well stocked shop and the best place to pick up advice. Talma also runs a **Windsurfing Academy** at the Silver Rock Hotel.

To return home, drive back up the hill to the church with the green roof, this time continuing straight on until you meet a roundabout. Take the first exit and follow the road which will take you back to Oistins. If you are heading to the west coast, drive to the next roundabout and take the right exit back to the ABC Highway.

Calendar of Special Events

Contact the Barbados Tourism Authority (BTA), tel: 427-2623, for further information on any of the events listed here.

JANUARY

The Barbados National Trust (BNT) launches its annual **Open House** program. Every Wednesday afternoon the Trust leads visitors into some of the island's most celebrated private homes not normally open to the public. They include the opulent, the architecturally unique and the historical. The program runs until early April. Tel: 436-9033 for details.

The Barbados Horticultural Society also hosts its **Open Gardens** program this month. Local enthusiasts open their private gardens to the public in the afternoons on one day a week. To find out where to go, tel: 428-5889.

Tropical ambience and an exciting mix of headliner names makes Barbados' annual **Paint It Jazz** festival a big hit. The five-day event during the second week of January features a marathon of concerts in both indoor and outdoor settings. Tel: 429-2084 or the BTA on 427-2623.

FEBRUARY

Barbados has a very active Horticultural Society. Each year it hosts a weekend **Flower Show and Competition** at its headquarters at Balls Plantation, Christ Church. The event showcases all manner of locally and regionally grown flora from massive displays to single plants. For details, tel: 428-5889.

A little over a week of festivities marks the landing of the first settlers in Barbados in the **Holetown Festival**, which hinges on the February 17 landing date. A packed slate of daily events ranges from free concerts to an open-air arts and crafts market. A fun, family-oriented, grass roots event.

MARCH/APRIL

The Sandy Lane Barbados Gold Cup Race on the first weekend in March is the island's premier horseracing event. This nine-furlong invitational race attracts class 'A' horses from Barbados and neighboring islands. The event draws a large crowd, a celebratory atmosphere and much pomp and ceremony.

Easter heralds the **Holder's Opera Season**, a young but highly popular three-week attraction. Internationally acclaimed singers and actors mingle with local performers in Shakespearean productions, operas and special concerts in the outdoor setting of the famed Holders Plantation House. Deviating from the main musical theme, the program also embraces polo, golf and cricket events.

Oistins Fish Festival, held in the fishing town of Oistins over the Easter Weekend, celebrates the island's fishing

One of many flights of fancy

industry in a host of mainly free events including a street fair and fish boning and other competitions highlighting fishing skills.

De Malibu Congaline Carnival, held the last week of April and culminating on May Day (May 1), is the island's newest 'street jam' festival. The formation of the region's longest Conga line, daily concerts, the daily Congaline Village of arts, crafts and local food, and the T-shirt band road march are a few of the highlights.

MAY/JUNE

Gospelfest, held during the latter part of May, is a weekend of gospel concerts featuring top local and international performers.

JULY/AUGUST

Crop Over, the island's biggest national festival, spreads over the entire month of July, culminating on the first Monday in August. This national celebration, one of the region's oldest festivals, heralded the end of the sugar crop and was traditionally characterised by feasting and dancing in the plantation yards (*see page 15*).

Today Crop Over features a daily slate of cultural, historical, and musical events. Much interest is focused

Crop Over gadfly

on calypso competitions that start in the 'tents' and progress through eliminations to the finals. On the last four days of the festival are the Pic-O-De-Crop Finals; Bridgetown Market (craft fair); Cohobbolo Pot, a variety show and the road march and costumed parade on Grand Kadooment Day.

The **Banks Hockey Festival** attracts teams from around the world. For information, tel: Will Alleyne 426-0909.

OCTOBER

Sun, Sea and Slams International Bridge Festival is an annual five-day bridge competition held around the middle of the month.

NOVEMBER

The year's major **international surfing competition** is traditionally held in November. The premier surfing event held at Bathsheba's 'Soup Bowl' tests the mettle of top regional and North American talent.

NIFCA (National Independence Festival of Creative Arts) celebrates the island's independence with a month of displays and competitions in all facets of the creative arts.

Barbados also celebrates independence with a program of community activities. Official ceremonies normally take place at the Garrison Savannah.

DECEMBER

Run Barbados is an annual international road race comprising two events, a 10km (6-mile) race and a 26-mile marathon. It is held in the first weekend in December.

Competing in 'Run Barbados'

Shopping

Barbados is no bargain basement, but you can find duty-free goods and local souvenirs at reasonable prices.

Duty Free

Barbados abounds in duty-free shopping. There are many small shops and department store branches in the tourist hubs but the widest selection by far is on Broad Street, Bridgetown's main drag. Lines of large department stores and specialty shops cram both sides of the street, offering everything from the world's finest china and electronic equipment to cashmere sweaters and internationally known skin-care products and toiletries.

With a bit of advance research, you might find items well below prices charged at home. However, duty-free does not automatically mean cheaper. If you have ideas about particular items that you would like to shop for, it is always sensible to check your home country prices first. Depending on the goods and where you are from, you may find what you want cheaper at home.

The bigger, multi-story department stores in Bridgetown are **Cave Shepherd** and **Harrisons**. Both have exhaustive (and exhausting) duty-free selections. Niche stores include **Colombian Emeralds International**, **Correia's**, **Little Switzerland** and the **Royal Shop**, which specialize in high quality jewelry. Little Switzerland also has an impressive range of camera and audio equipment.

You can only buy duty-free if you present your passport and return ticket, so don't forget to take them when you go shopping. You can take most items with you at the time of purchase, but you

All that glitters

69

still have to pick up tobacco, alcohol and a few other items at the airport.

Rum

The island is vastly experienced in rum production so you will find wide selections and excellent value for money just about anywhere, including duty-free shops, virtually all tourist shopping centers and even in the supermarkets.

Rum products range from 'white' or clear rums to very dark rums, and from 'young' rums to well-aged. There are also specialty rum products, such as Malibu White Rum with Coconut, as well as rum brandies and creams. Principal local names include Mount Gay, which operates the world's oldest distillery, established in 1703; Cockspur, Doorly's and a white rum line from E.S.A. Field, a subsidiary of Doorly's. Each line has a number of products based on age, color and proof; watch your labels, as a few of these rums go heavily into 'overproof.'

Arts and Crafts

Barbados is blossoming with local artists and there are several private galleries that offer a good sampling of what is around. In many instances you may be able to contact a local artist directly. The best known – and most commercial – outlet is the **Best of Barbados** chain of shops, offering an entire line of mass-produced items imprinted with the works of Jill Walker.

For more personal tastes, you can view a wide range of work at the **Barbados Arts Council** shop in Pelican Village on Harbour Road just outside Bridgetown. This cluster of shops is also a fruitful source of handicrafts in wood, coral and other media.

Fresh from the kiln

There are many other private galleries, including the **Verandah Gallery** (upstairs Collins Pharmacy, Broad Street), reflecting local and regional culture and lifestyle; **Mango's**, Speightstown – featuring silk screens by Michael Adams; **Gang of 4 Art Studio**, Speightstown and **The Art Foundry** at Heritage Park. The largest of all, with the widest selection of Caribbean and local art, is **The Kirby Gallery**, Hastings (open Monday to Friday 10am–6pm; Saturday 10am–2pm; tel: 430-3032).

For locally produced handicrafts, **Pelican Village** on Harbour Road just outside Bridgetown, sells basketry, woodwork, jewelry and more; or try the **Chattel Village** in St Lawrence Gap. By far the best collection of arts and crafts can be found at local fairs and festivals. Scan the press for current events.

Mahogany is a slow-growing tropical hardwood that has beautiful texture and color. **Medford's Craft Village**, located just north of Bridgetown, is a shopping expedition in itself. You'll find just about everything that can possibly be fashioned from mahogany and other woods and you can watch the workers shaping the products on the spot. If you're not able to get to Medford's, a limited range of their products are found in most tourist shops.

For batik a good bet is **John C. Mayers Batiks**, Bathsheba, St Joseph. Other hand-painted art works, mostly in the form of clothing, can be purchased from **Colours of de Caribbean** in Bridgetown. Look out for locally produced swimsuits from **Sandbox Designs** and hand-painted soft furnishings under the **Mango Jam** label.

For pottery, **Earthworks** in Edghill Heights, St Thomas sells tableware and household items that reflect Caribbean style. **Painted Earth** features unusual hand-painted ceramics which can also be found at **The Monkey Pot** shops in Pelican Village and St Lawrence Gap.

Antiques

Antique shops dot the shopping areas, especially around Holetown. While fascinating to browse through, for the most part items in these stores are grossly overpriced. But you just might find a quaint curio in your price-range. **Antiquaria** is a long-standing name with branches in Holetown and Fontabelle, just outside Bridgetown. Another antique shop worth trying is **La Gallerie Antique** just before Holetown.

'Jamming' T-shirt motif

T-shirts

The T-shirt industry thrives on Barbados. Many items are made from the silkier textured sea island cotton, and quality is generally high. Try **Irie Blue** and **Ganzee** stores or **Cave Shepherd**.

Eating Out

The long-standing British influence coupled with a subsistence life whose diet was based primarily on ground provisions kept Barbados almost bereft of creative culinary flair for centuries. But tourism attracted international-class chefs and brought overseas training for locals, and these two developments helped alter the face of Barbados' menus. Creative cuisine now abounds, and the emphasis is on the use of local ingredients to make award-winning dishes.

The national dish is flying fish and *cou cou*. Flying fish is wholly Barbados' own. Small and quite delicate and tasty when not over-cooked or too heavily seasoned, it is served many ways including fried, steamed and roasted. *Cou cou*, an adaptation of the West African 'foo-foo' vegetable dish, is a side dish of mashed corn meal and okra beaten until smooth. Chicken is enjoyed in every form and fashion and is popular in *roti*, a folded pastry with a savory filling. Other little side dishes include breadfruit, a starchy fruit often prepared like potatoes, but especially delicious pickled, and plantain, a banana-like fruit that is sliced and fried. It has a slightly sweet flavor, yet is compatible with a savory meal.

Fruits of the sea

Pudding and souse, once known as a 'poor man's food,' are wholly Barbadian. Assumed to have come from the plantation days, they evolved into popular dishes traditionally eaten on Saturday. Made from pig's intestines, black pudding also utilizes some of the pig's blood while white pudding does not. Souse is pickled pig's head or feet.

Steak fish is popular, especially king fish and dolphin (not the 'Flipper' kind, but dorado). There are also several types of 'red' fish, such as snapper, a seasonal fish found in late summer. The indigenous Black Belly sheep is finding its way onto restaurant menus these days, usually fried, baked or grilled.

Barbados shines in the drinks arena, particularly drinks that utilize rum or rum products. Favorites include the age-old rum punch or Planter's punch, a very smooth drink with a surprising kick, so beware. The recipe calls for 'one sour' (lime), 'two sweet' (sugar), 'three strong' (rum) and 'four weak' (water). Punch à creme is a Christmas version, using eggs, milk, rum and bitters. Also at Christ-

Preparing sorrel

mas you may hear about Falernum, a traditional drink made from lime and white rum, which is boiled to a syrupy consistency then bottled and fermented.

Mauby, a bark soaked in spices, is an acquired taste, with bite. More appealing perhaps is ginger beer, made from ginger and lime. While it can be bought bottled, it is often homemade. Sorrel is a spicy traditional Christmas drink: the dried sepals of the sorrel plant are steeped in spices such as cinnamon and cloves and served with or without rum added.

The island's best known beer is Banks, which has won international awards. Coconut water is available in most bars, but also from roadside vendors, who will cut your coconut for you and serve it with a straw. They will also slash open the coconut if you want the 'jelly' – the soft part that is just beginning to solidify.

There are nearly as many places to eat on Barbados as there are places to stay. But bear in mind that many ingredients are imported or, when not available, substitutions are made, so not all foreign cuisines are entirely authentic. But Barbados has something special: a bevy of international-class chefs. While most are found in the finer hotels, others have opened their own restaurants.

Barbados is not a cheap place to dine out. While it boasts many fast food eateries along the south and west coasts, you will find even these can run high – and not very fast, either.

But there are good, value-for-money fast food establishments and restaurants to be found, and when it comes to economical dining the south coast reigns. Don't forget the gourmet sandwich places such as **Kitchen Korner** in Holetown and **The Lunch Club** in Hastings.

This selection is by no means complete (*see Nightlife, page 77* for other choices). For a guide to prices (in US dollars per person, meal only) including 15 percent tax: Inexpensive ($) = under $20; Moderate ($$) = $20–40; Expensive ($$$) = $40–60.

Bridgetown and Environs

THE BOATYARD
Bay Street, Bridgetown
Tel: 436-2622
A bubbling bistro atmosphere with great beach close to town. $

BROWN SUGAR
Aquatic Gap, Bay St
Tel: 426-7684
West Indian dishes with an excellent, value-for-money buffet lunch. $–$$

JEFF MEX
Broad St, Bridgetown
Tel: 431-0857
Popular Mexican fare. $

MUSTOR'S
McGregor St, Bridgetown
Tel: 426-5175
Bajan food no frills. Lunch only. $

RUSTY PELICAN
Cavans Lane, Bridgetown
Tel: 436-7778
Excellent place on the Careenage. $$

WATERFRONT CAFÉ
The Careenage, Bridgetown
Tel: 427-0093
An established favorite serving Caribbean and continental dishes. $$

Weighing in
West Coast

BOMBAS
Paynes Bay, St James
Tel: 432-0569
A west coast favorite with a lively atmosphere and creative dishes. Daily specials. $

CARAMBOLA
Derricks, St James
Tel: 432-0832
An oceanfront setting and fine food make this a popular choice. $$$

THE CLIFF
Derricks, St James
Tel: 432-1922
Elegant restaurant often awarded top billing for delicious food, good service and style. $$$

COCOMOS
Holetown, St James
Tel: 432-0134
Colorfully and creatively decorated with lots of Caribbean flavor. $-$$

FATHOMS
Paynes Bay, St James
Tel: 432-2568
Fish specialties with a waterfront setting. Lunch and dinner only; closed Sunday. $$

FISHERMANS PUB
Speightstown, St Peter
Tel: 422-2703
A pleasant beach side location and lively spot. $

ILE DE FRANCE
Settlers Beach Hotel, St James
Tel: 422-3245
Fine French food and hospitality. $$–$$$

Sensational seafood

THE LONE STAR GARAGE
Mount Standfast, St James
Tel: 419-0599
Stylishly casual and elegant. Serves both baked beans and caviar. $$–$$$

THE MEWS
Holetown, St James
Tel: 432-1122
Olde-worlde ambiance; friendly service and gourmet dishes. $$–$$$

NICO'S WINE BAR
Derricks, St James
Tel: 432-6386
A successful wine bar with a loyal clientele. $$

OLIVES BAR & BISTRO
Holetown, St James
Tel: 432-2112
A charming, quality place. $$–$$$

SAKURA
Holetown, St James
Tel: 432-5187
The island's only Japanese restaurant. Excellent. $$–$$$

South Coast

CAFÉ SOL
St Lawrence Gap, Christ Church
Tel: 435-9531
Hearty Mexican dishes; crowded. $$

CARIB BEACH BAR
Worthing, Christ Church
Tel: 435-8540
Superb location, a local favorite. $

CHAMPERS
Hastings, Christ Church
Tel: 435-6644
A super bistro on the waterfront with an innovative menu. $$

JOSEF'S
St Lawrence Gap, Christ Church
Tel: 435-8245
By far the finest restaurant in this area. European cuisine. $$–$$$

McBRIDES
St Lawrence Gap, Christ Church
Tel: 435-6352
A bustling Irish bar popular with young British visitors. $$

East Coast

ATLANTIS HOTEL
Bathsheba, St Joseph
Tel: 433-9445
Excellent Sunday buffet; hearty meals every day. $

Try Tex-Mex at Café Sol

BONITO BAR
Bathsheba, St Joseph
Tel: 433-9034
A rustic surfing hangout. $

ROUND HOUSE
Bathsheba, St Joseph
Tel: 433-9678
A busy pub overlooking the sea. $–$$

Nightlife

Nightlife in Barbados is highly varied, and there is no shortage of things to do. Music runs the gamut, from country and western and 'oldies' to dub and soca. For many years the island was not especially well known for its musical prowess but in the early 1990s several groups and artistes burst onto the regional and international scene simultaneously and now much of the region follows Barbados' lead. You should be able to sample some of this fine talent during your stay.

Many of the larger hotels provide floor shows, live music and other local acts, entertainment often staged during dinner. However, if you want to get out and experience a bit more local flavor, then you will definitely be looking at a late night experience. While you can have an early night and still have fun, unlike many of the other islands where the streets practically roll up after dinner, in Barbados the action doesn't start until 11pm, particularly on the south coast.

An addition to traditional local nightlife is the 'sports bar', with satellite television. In Worthing there is Bubba's, The Lucky Horseshoe Saloon which opens 24-hours and Bert's Bar at Abbeville Hotel. Further up the coast is McBrides in St Lawrence Gap and on the west coast Crocodile's Den. (*see West Coast listings page 79*).

South Coast to Bridgetown

The south coast, particularly the St Lawrence Gap strip and a short Bay Street stretch just before Bridgetown, teems with action well into the small hours. You will find everything here from elaborate floor shows to outdoor fish fries where people gather for an impromptu bite to eat.

THE BOATYARD

Bay Street, Bridgetown
Tel: 436-2622
A popular drinking spot where you can hear live bands several nights a week. This is a large open-air complex that hosts a variety of events. Call ahead for a current schedule of what's on.

Jazz at the Waterfront Café

HARBOUR LIGHTS
Bay Street, Bridgetown
Tel: 436-7225
A popular late-night hangout and dance spot attracting a young to early middle-age crowd. Located on Carlisle Bay beach, it has a pleasant open-air setting, elevated dance floor and food on sale. There is a DJ and sometimes live acts. Cover charges vary. Action doesn't start before 11pm.

WATERFRONT CAFÉ
The Careenage
Tel: 427-0093
This restaurant offers frequent jazz acts

Music man

and steelpan music by night. Dress is a little more upscale than in other south coast venues. Sit at a table on the sidewalk and take in the picturesque harbor or take a spin around the dance floor.

B4 BLUES
St Lawrence Gap, Christ Church
Tel: 435-6560
A funky little place in the Gap with a popular blues night. Busy on the weekends

with a variety of music. Good bistro with international cuisine.

PLANTATION RESTAURANT/ TROPICAL SPECTACULAR
St Lawrence Main Road, Christ Church
Tel: 428-5048
This is a glittering cabaret performance of Caribbean music, culture and dance. You can also dine to the sounds of a live steel band music and dance the night away to the sounds of top local talent. Performances on Wednesday and Friday. Call for details.

OISTINS FISH MARKET
A crowded hot spot, particularly on Friday nights. The casual outdoor setting and pumping music coupled with delicious fresh fish (prepared local-style while you wait) attract locals and visitors into the early morning.

THE SHIP INN
St Lawrence Gap, Christ Church
Tel: 435-6961
This long-standing venue in the Gap sets the pace for others to follow. It deftly sails a course between pub/restaurant and bar/nightclub. The Ship is the island's only establishment with live entertainment every night and showcases a variety of local talent.

MCBRIDES
St Lawrence Gap, Christ Church
Tel: 435-6352
This lively Irish pub is packed most nights of the week. It features DJ music and small live acts; popular with 20-somethings and British visitors.

REGGAE LOUNGE
St Lawrence Gap, Christ Church
Tel: 435-6462
A rustic open-air nightclub. The bar is at the top entrance level and there are steps down to the dancefloor below. Occasionally hosts live reggae acts but most nights has DJ music.

West Coast

Lower key than the island's south coast, the west coast offers a more refined night life.

MV Harbour Master logo

THE MEWS
Holetown, St James
Tel: 432-1122
Friday nights feature a talented local jazz duo, and the intimate atmosphere attracts an upscale crowd.

NICO'S WINE BAR
Derricks, St James
Tel: 432-6386
Although principally a restaurant, Nico's hosts some live entertainment and is a popular meeting spot on the west coast. Enjoy the warm friendly atmosphere or perhaps play one of the games available from the bar.

CROCODILE'S DEN
Payne's Bay, St James
Tel: 432-7625
The place to go very late at night or early in the morning! Your host, Harry Hinds, has an extensive record collection and plays requests. There are also lots of games to entertain customers including pool tables, game machines, air-hockey and table tennis. Relaxed ambiance.

COACH HOUSE
Paynes Bay
St James
Tel: 432-1163
Styled on a typical English pub. Extensively refurbished, it hosts live bands and more.

BOURBON STREET
Prospect, St James
Tel: 424-4557
New Orleans-influenced restaurant with live jazz and blues on Friday and weekend nights. Parking can be difficult.

CASBAH
Baku Beach, St James
Tel: 432-1872
Moroccan themed nightclub at the Baku complex. Saturday is the big night. Attracts a cross-section of age groups.

East Coast

ROUND HOUSE
Bathsheba, St Joseph
Tel: 433-9678
Rock, reggae and jazz in a spectacular location, and good food too. Take a jacket as it gets cool in the evening.

PRACTICAL information

GETTING THERE

Most visitors enter Barbados by air unless they are passing through for the day on a cruise ship. The island has one airport, **Grantley Adams International**, at the south end of the island. The airport operates 24 hours a day and has one of the longest runways in the region. It has a small inbound duty-free shopping outlet and a Tourism Authority information booth in the arrivals hall. A good taxi service operates from just outside the departure lounge.

Barbados is served by several international and regional carriers. British West Indian Airways (BWIA) International flies a regular service between Barbados and

Landing in paradise

several North American and European destinations, including Miami, New York, and London.

American Airlines operates daily between Barbados and Puerto Rico, Miami and New York. Air Canada flies direct from Montreal and Toronto.

British Airways and Caledonian fly regularly into Barbados from the UK, and Concorde flies to Barbados in the winter. Other European points are serviced by LTU, Condor and MartinAir.

South America connects to Barbados by Guyana Airways and the inter-island carrier LIAT (Leeward Island Air Transport). Along with LIAT, several regional charters link the island to other Caribbean islands, and several international charters fly to Barbados from European and North American destinations in the winter season. Have your travel agent check the options from your destination to determine best fares and travel times.

Barbados is a primary port of call in the Caribbean and several cruise lines make day stops year round.

TRAVEL ESSENTIALS

Passports/Visas

Everyone entering Barbados should hold a valid passport and return ticket. Although United States and Canadian citizens can enter with just a photo ID and an original or certified birth certificate, passports are required on leaving and re-entering the US. Make sure you know with whom and where you are staying in Barbados, as you are likely to be asked.

Visas are required for citizens from Eastern European nations, Russia, most Asian and Arab countries, the People's Republic of China, Taiwan, India, Japan, Pakistan, non-Commonwealth countries of Africa, Guatemala, Honduras, Haiti and all South American countries except Argentina, Brazil, Colombia and Venezuela.

Check the nearest consulate or your travel agent, as the visa list can change.

Vaccinations

No vaccinations are required for entry into Barbados.

Customs

Customs may ask you to open your luggage for a search, which is not uncommon. Most customs officers are pleasant and reasonable, and after a quick look, will send you on your way.

Customs limits are 200 cigarettes or 50 cigars, 1 liter of spirits.

Barbados frowns on the importation of plant matter, fresh produce and certain other unprocessed perishable goods. If you must bring something of this nature, check with the nearest Barbados Consulate or tourism office on the current regulations. When you arrive there is an agriculture counter where these items are examined.

Pets

Barbados is one of a handful of rabies-free nations. Importation of any rabies-prone pet from anywhere in the world (other than England) must first go through a six-month quarantine in the United Kingdom.

Climate

Barbados has a consistent year-round tropical climate, with temperatures averaging 84–88°F (29–31°C) during the day and 75–79°F (24–26°C) at night. Trade winds cool the island most of the year.

While the island enjoys some 3,000 hours of sun annually, June to November is the official hurricane (rainy) season. The first few months usually bring little more than the occasional rainy spell but in September and October storm activity in

the region is at a peak. Barbados has not had a hurricane since 1955, but weather systems that bring days of rain are most frequent during this period.

The dry season is December to June, when, except for sudden sharp showers that quickly pass, the sun reigns.

Clothing

Barbados is a tropical climate, so humidity is higher than in the temperate zones. For this reason you should bring lightweight clothing made from material that breathes, such as cotton, linen and other natural fibers.

Casual apparel is fine for the day and most evenings. However, one should re-

Cool lady

spect the local population by refraining from wearing beachwear and skimpy clothing in public places.

Evening wear can be dressy if you plan to dine out or enjoy a floor show. Sport shirts for men and light dresses for women are acceptable, although some of the more exclusive restaurants require men to wear a jacket and tie. Most night clubs do not allow men to wear hats or vests. Shoes and shirts are required in all public places.

During winter the night air can be cool, so a light sweater or wrap is advisable.

Electricity

The electricity in Barbados is dependable and steady. Barbados operates on the odd system of 110 volts/50 cycles, but most 60 cycle items work here. The typical North American two-prong plug is used throughout the island and many hotels have 220 volt outlets in the bathrooms.

Time Zone

Barbados is in the United States Eastern Standard time zone, four hours behind Greenwich Mean Time. It does not operate Daylight Savings Time.

GETTING ACQUAINTED

Geography

Shaped something like a pear, Barbados is a mere 14 miles (22km) wide by 21 miles (34km) long. The most easterly of the Caribbean chain, this 166-sq-mile (429-sq-km) island is a relatively flat, coral-capped island compared to its volcanic

Geography lesson

neighbors. Though lacking the sharply crested terrain of the other islands, Barbados has a character all its own. The brisk, cosmopolitan texture of Bridgetown and other urban centers combines with the gentle charm of undulating greenery and colorful rows of quaint chattel house villages.

About one-sixth of the island, in the Scotland District in the northeast, is dramatically jagged with a terrain of clay and sedimentary deposits. Much of the pre-history of the island chain is readily visible in these rocky formations.

The island's tallest point is 1,100-ft (336-meter) Mount Hillaby in St Thomas, just north of the island center.

Government/Economy

Barbados enjoys one of the oldest parliamentary systems in the world (its first representative body was formed in 1639). Unlike other islands, it remained peacefully in the hands of the British until November 30, 1966, when it gained independence.

Barbados operates under a democratic parliamentary system, or a constitutional monarchy, with the island's Governor General representing the monarchy as head of state. The Senate and House of Assembly are headed by the Prime Minister. There are two principal political parties which represent 28 constituencies.

The economy is driven by sugar and tourism. For centuries sugar was the island's main revenue earner, but in the early 1980s tourism usurped it as the main foreign exchange earner. While winter is known as the high season for tourism, traditional patterns are changing due to the high number of budget travelers arriving on charter flights during the summer months. A strong off-shore financial sector has helped diversify the economy making it one of the strongest and most stable in the Caribbean.

Population

Barbados is one of the most densely populated islands in the region with some 260,000 inhabitants. More than 90 percent of the population is of African descent, with principal minority populations comprising Caucasian, East Indian and Syrian/Lebanese.

Religion

More than 100 denominations and sects thrive, the largest being Anglican. Other religions include Roman Catholic, Baptist, Christian Science, Jewish, Methodist, Moravian, Muslim and Pentecostal.

Language/Dialect

On first hearing locals talk, you may well ask yourself if it is English they are speaking. It is. Bajan dialect is very colorful and expressive with many nuances and short-cuts. Most notable is the habit of clipping off the end consonant of words. 'Helping' verbs are rarely used in dialect,

so instead of 'I have gone' or 'I will go' you will hear 'I gone.' The 'th' sound is generally clipped to either a 't' or 'd' sound, so 'that' becomes 'dat' and 'youth' become 'yute.' If you are interested in this subject pick up a copy of Frank Collymore's *Bajan Dialect* at local bookstores.

MONEY MATTERS

Currency

Barbados carries its own currency, the Barbados dollar, which is tied to the US dollar. The exchange rate is set at BDS $1.98 to US$1, and this is the rate (plus some fees) you will get in the banks and most stores. However, the street rate is a straight two to one, and it is common to mix currencies when dealing with ancillary services such as taxis.

Credit Cards

Major credit cards are readily accepted in restaurants, stores, hotels and most shops catering to visitors.

Banking

Banks usually require customers to show their passport and ticket when exchanging foreign currency in either direction. Local laws prevent Barbadians from obtaining foreign currency above a certain limit, so it is standard procedure to show these items, particularly if you are changing local money into your own currency. You may need a passport when getting cash advances on your credit card.

ATM machines that will dispense local currency against your credit card are en-countered island-wide. Virtually all these machines require a PIN (Personal Identification Number), so unless you have a card with a PIN, you will have to exchange your money inside the bank. As a rule, bank hours are Monday to Thursday 8am–3pm, and Friday 8am–5pm.

Tipping

Bajans love to be tipped. From the time you step into the arrivals hall and the porters (Red Caps) begin hounding you for your luggage, tips will be expected. Red Caps are entitled to BDS$1 per bag. People tend to tip higher, but if a Red Cap tries to insist on more, you needn't feel obliged to give it.

Check your bill carefully at restaurants to see if a service charge has been included. If not, a 10–15 percent tip is the norm.

Departure Tax

The departure tax is BDS$25 and is not usually included in travel packages.

GETTING AROUND

By Bus

The cheapest, and certainly most elbow-rubbing, way to get around the island is by bus. The bus system is partially privatized, so the urban districts are flooded with a host of PSVs (public service vehicles). There are large government buses, squat yellow mini-buses, 'maxi taxis' and small vans (ZM and ZR plates) all along the south and west coast stretches. There is a standard flat fare, but you must have the exact change on government buses.

Local mini-bus

For buzzing up and down your particular stretch of coast or popping into Bridgetown, any of the PSVs will do, and since there are so many your wait will be short. But because all transport emanates from Bridgetown with little cross-country movement, travel in rural areas is time-consuming. It means a trip into Bridgetown, then walking the length of the city to change terminals and quite often a long wait before departure.

In the country, buses are rarely on time and waits at stops can be irritatingly long.

By Car

Renting a car offers greater independence than using public transport and Barbados has more than 60 auto rental companies offering everything from little convertible mini mokes to air-conditioned vans. Rates are flat and most of the rental agents issue local licenses off your home license (US $5) along with delivery and 24-hour emergency service.

Although Barbados is small, driving on the **left** side of its meandering 900 miles (1,450km) or so of narrow roads is a challenge for some. Besides getting lost, which is a given, the 30mph (50kph) speed limit seems fast when learning to share the road with bicycles, donkey carts, pedestrians and push carts laden with anything from 20-ft (6-meter) boards to piles of chairs. Luxuries like sidewalks and shoulders are seen only on the few real highways, where speed limits are 50mph (80kpm).

The most important thing to remember when driving on Barbados is to stay alert and on the left. In the country, hug your side of the road and announce yourself at every corner by honking the horn. Cars can be rented at about US $200–300 per week depending on the size and features of the vehicle. **Corbins Garage** in Collymore Rock (tel: 427-9531) has one of the largest and most reliable fleets on the island. Prices are the same year-round and you can drop the car at the airport when you leave.

Stoute's Rentals in Christ Church (tel: 435-4456) has a good fleet of sturdy vehicles, and **Top Car Rentals** in Christ Church (tel: 435-0378) offers good service and reasonable year-round prices. In high season make arrangements in advance as vehicles quickly become scarce.

Be careful when considering bicycle or motorbike rental, as they can prove dangerous on shoulderless roads and some companies do not carry insurance.

Taxis are everywhere and while pricey

Freewheeler

as a regular means of transport are recommended at night if you are not renting your own vehicle or wish to try a restaurant outside your area and plan to consume alcohol. Rates are fixed by destination, but it is always advisable to agree on the fare in advance of setting off. Up to five persons can travel in a taxi at no extra charge.

HOURS & HOLIDAYS

Business Hours

Most stores are open from 8am–4pm on weekdays and on Saturday morning. The larger supermarkets usually stay open until 9pm on Friday. Some mini marts and Bridgetown pharmacies also open on Sunday mornings.

Public Holidays

New Year's Day; Errol Barrow Day (January 21); Good Friday; Easter Monday; Heroes Day (April 28); May Day (May 1); Whit Monday (varies each year); Emancipation Day (August 1); Kadooment Day (first Monday of August); United Nations Day (first Monday of October); Independence Day (November 30); Christmas Day and Boxing Day (December 25 and 26).

BEACHES

Barbados has many long stretches of good beach as well as tucked-away coves nestling between rocky shorelines. While most of the west coast starting from Brighton and extending up to Speightstown is packed with good beaches, among the very best is **Paradise Beach** at the south edge of St James. Though Paradise Hotel which flanks the beach is closed, you can enjoy this lovely spot by the public access on the south end of the property.

Sandy Lane Bay is where the island's five-star hotel stands, it is a wonderful beach; public access is at the south end of the property.

A little north of Holetown a road on the north side of Colony Club offers public access to one of my favorite beaches in front of the famous **Heron Bay House**, a wonderful, little-known stop. When you're swimming here, watch out for the spiny 'cobblers' (black sea urchins), because touching or scraping their spines is very painful.

Mullins Bay in St Peter, just in front of the restaurant, has a good beach, and **Heywoods Beach**, next to Almond Beach Village in St Peter, is also a good bet in the north. While the northern St Peter and St Lucy beaches are lovely to look at, the undertows and currents here are ferocious. In fact, it is best not to swim anywhere along the Atlantic side of the island, with the exception of **Bath** in St John where the currents are less intense and lifeguards are usually posted. **Crane Beach** in St Philip is sometimes safe, so inquire first. **Long Bay**, also in St Philip, has a beautiful beach tucked away between the jagged coral ledges.

As with all beaches, but in particular the entire north and eastern Atlantic sides, never swim alone and always heed local warnings. What looks safe could prove treacherous.

At the bottom of the island is **Round Rock**, also called **Silver Rock Beach**. This is a lovely wide beach, excellent for wind surfing, but it also packs a powerful undertow. Consider this strip as potentially tricky as the north and east, and follow local advice on current conditions. On the south coast before Oistins is **Enterprise** or **Miami Beach**, a fairly sheltered and popular beach.

Most beaches north of Oistins are appealing, but a few stand out. At the south end of St Lawrence Gap is **Dover Beach**, a popular spot with many facilities. **Accra**, or **Rockley Beach**, is one of the island's most popular beaches because it is wide and long and has a good range of facilities.

Sand, sea and sails, Dover Beach

ACCOMMODATION

If you are looking for a place to stay, Barbados has hundreds of choices. They range from the sophisticated luxury hotels (US $400+ per night) mainly found on the west coast to basic guest houses and privately owned cottages. All-inclusive hotels are also popular. An accommodation listing can be found at Barbados Tourism Offices *(see page 89).*

During the summer (late April to October), when rain is expected more frequently, you can expect a steep drop in prices compared to what you would pay in the winter months. The prices indicated here are based on a room for two during high season (winter: November to April).

$ = under US$100; $$ = US$100–150;
$$$ = US$150–250.

South Coast

The south coast is the favored area for value-for-money stays. Crammed with activity from Accra Beach to the far end of St Lawrence Gap. What this shore lacks in serenity it makes up for in convenience.

Large Hotels

ACCRA BEACH HOTEL
Worthing, Christ Church
Tel: 435-8920
Large quiet complex; close to Bridgetown; popular with business travelers. $$

CASAURINA BEACH CLUB
St Lawrence Gap Christ Church
Tel: 428-3600
Family atmosphere; rooms with kitchenette; beautiful gardens and local touches. $$$.

Table for two

COCONUT COURT
Worthing, Christ Church
Tel: 427-1655
Young and lively with recreational rooms and friendly staff. Good value. $–$$

SANDY BEACH HOTEL
Worthing, Christ Church
Tel: 435-8000
Good value, pleasant rooms with kitchenette; spectacular beach. $$.

TIME OUT AT THE GAP
St Lawrence Gap, Christ Church
Tel: 420-5021
Cheap and cheerful. Pool, bar and cable TV; air-conditioned rooms. $

Small Hotels

ABBEVILLE HOTEL
Rockley, Christ Church
Tel: 435-7924
A good low-cost bet. Close to beach. $

BAGSHOT HOUSE
Worthing, Christ Church
Tel: 435-6956
Pleasant family-run establishment; breakfast included; on excellent beach. $

LITTLE BAY HOTEL
Worthing, Christ Church
Tel: 435-7246
Charming with a good restaurant; close to beach and shops. $–$$

Aparthotels/Villas

MAGIC ISLE
Worthing, Christ Church
Tel: 435-6760
Well-equipped kitchen; balcony to sea. $$

SEA FOAM HACIENDAS
Worthing, Christ Church
Tel: 435-7380
Well-equipped kitchen; balcony to sea. $$

Guest Houses

CRYSTAL WATERS
Worthing, Christ Church
Tel: 435-7514
Basic with own shower; on Sandy Beach. $

SHELL'S GUEST HOUSE
Worthing, Christ Church
Tel: 435-7253
Basic room, shared bathroom; near beach with small friendly bistro. $

West Coast

The west coast has the most upscale hotels on the island. However, if you are on a budget, apartment hotels with your own cooking facilities or all-inclusive hotels are the way to go. Remember summer rates can make the luxury hotels more affordable.

Apartments

EUROPA APARTMENTS
Sunset Crest, St James
Tel: 432-6750
Inexpensive; young guests; close to beach. $

INN ON THE BEACH
Holetown, St James
Tel: 432-0385
Family run; close to shops. $$

SMUGGLERS' COVE
Paynes Bay, St James
Tel: 432-1741
Only 20 units at this reserved property on a beautiful beach. $$

All-Inclusive Resorts
MANGO BAY
Holetown, St James
Tel: 432-1384
Charming property with pool; friendly staff. $$$$

THE REGENT ST JAMES
Holetown, St James
Tel: 432-6666
Newly appointed premises; convenient location. $$$

East Coast
This coast offers visitors a different perspective of Barbados. The pounding seas and wind, and rugged coastline have made it a surfers' paradise. Its quaint coastal villages are home to real country folk. This area is far removed from the capital and other attractions; it is likely you will need to hire a car.

Hotels
CRANE BEACH HOTEL
St Philip
Tel: 423-6220
Oceanfront setting with clifftop views. Rooms with antique furnishing. $$

EDGEWATER HOTEL
Bathsheba, St Joseph
Tel: 433-9900
Old-world rustic atmosphere with breathtaking cliff-top view. $

Pool at Crane Beach

ROUND HOUSE
Bathsheba, St Joseph
Tel: 433-9678
Elegant 19th-century building; only 5 well appointed rooms; delightful setting. $

HEALTH

The standard of health facilities is relatively high in Barbados. There are two hospitals, Queen Elizabeth (government-run) and Bayview (private). QEH is a 600-bed facility with several specialized services, an emergency room and a rather slow ambulance service. The Barbados Defense Force also operates an ambulance in dire situations. There are several polyclinics island-wide and a large representation of private medical practitioners, specialists, dentists and pharmacies.

Barbados has a decompression chamber for diving mishaps, operated by the Barbados Defense Force.

Medical insurance from recognized insurance plans is sometimes accepted at private facilities, but you should verify this. The QEH does not as a rule accept overseas medical plans, nor does it take credit cards.

PERSONAL SAFETY

Barbados is not a crime-prone destination, but like anywhere else, crime does exist. Visitors often tend to relax usual personal safety precautions on vacation and this is a mistake. Always secure your valuables and be alert. Most accommodations have house or room safes. Don't leave valuables unattended on the beaches or in vehicles. Certain areas are not safe to walk in at night, so check with your hotel staff first.

SPORTS

The national passion is cricket, and throughout the year there are amateur and professional matches taking place. Test and other matches are played at the fa-

Still waters

mous Kensington Oval (tel: 436-1397), which dates back to 1882.

Football (soccer) and horse racing are also popular. The local horse racing season is January to March and May to October. All races are held at the Garrison Savannah (contact the Barbados Turf Club, tel: 426-3980).

Barbados is also one of the world's top windsurfing destinations. It has the enviable reputation of being both an excellent flat water and wave destination. Surfing is also very big, particularly at the East Coast 'soup bowl.'

COMMUNICATIONS & NEWS

Newspapers

Barbados has two daily newspapers, *The Nation* and *The Advocate*. There is also a fortnightly regional paper, *Caribbean Week*. Two visitor publications come out every two weeks, *The Visitor* and *The Sunseeker,* and are free at most tourist outlets. There are a few annual visitor guides, *Barbados in a Nutshell*, which is free at many tourist centers, and *The Ins and Outs of Barbados*, which is often found free in guest rooms. Foreign publications are readily available throughout the island.

Television & Radio

There is one government-run television station, CBC (Caribbean Broadcasting Corporation), although most hotels have satellite dishes giving them access to North American programming. Subscription cable services are available locally.

There are several radio stations. CBC operates two: 900AM and Liberty 98.1FM which is probably the most popular local channel. Starcom network also has a number of stations including Hot 95.3, Yess 104.1FM and VOB (Voice of Barbados) 790AM. There is also a privately run religious station Faith102.1.

Most of the larger hotels offer fax services, and there are at least three Internet servers on the island.

Postal Information

There are post offices in every parish. The island's main post office is on the edge of Bridgetown. Most hotels and tourist outlets carry stamps and postcards, and your hotel will most likely post mail on your behalf. You will also find bright red postal slots in guard walls, the sides of buildings and other strange locations. Rest assured they are cleared each day so your mail is safe.

Telephones

The country code is (246).
Barbados has a reliable, island-wide phone service called Bartel. It is linked to the United States DDD (Direct Distance Dialing) system, so credit card calls can be made direct.

Coin-operated phone booths are located throughout the island, but they have a three-minute limit and tend to have long lines of people waiting to use them. You can buy phone cards, which allow you to speak for as long as you like, at Cave Shepherd on Broad Street in Bridgetown and any Bartel office. They come in denominations of BDS $10, $20, $40 and $60. However, phone card facilities are limited to only a few locations so are not very convenient. Call Bartel, tel: 434-2273 for the list.

Cellular phones can be used; have yours programed or rent one through Cellcom at 434-CELL. You can also utilize video

A quiet place to talk

conferencing and other high-tech facilities through Barbados External Telecommunications (BET), tel: 427-5200.

ATTRACTIONS

Cruising
Sail the Caribbean waters by day or night. A large number of boats are operated by Tall Ships (tel: 430-0900) such as the pirate boat *Jolly Roger* which has fun cruises or the steamboat-style *Harbour Master*. Private catamaran charters are available on *Cool Runnings* (tel: 436-0911) or on *Heat Wave* (tel: 423-7871). If you prefer a traditional vessel, champagne cruises are offered by *Stiletto* and *Regent I*; contact the Barbados Yacht Club, tel: 427-1125.

Aboard MV Harbour Master

National Trust Walks
These are real treats, not just because they give you an opportunity to see the island in the company of knowledgeable guides, but also because they are free. Hike Barbados is a year-round Sunday activity with 6am and 3pm 5-mile (8-km) hikes at three speeds; the leisurely stop 'n' stare, a medium pace, and the fast-paced grin and bear it. At full moon a moonlight hike starts at 5.30pm. Contact the Trust at tel: 436-9033.

USEFUL NUMBERS

Emergencies
Police: 211
Fire: 211
Ambulance service (Queen Elizabeth Hospital): 511
Queen Elizabeth Hospital (Public), Martindale's Road, St Michael: 436-6450
Bayview Hospital (private), St Paul's Avenue, Bayville, St Michael: 436-5446

Credit Card and Travelers' Check representatives
American Express: Lost or stolen cards: 800-327-1267; Travelers' checks: 800-221-7282
MasterCard: 800-307-7309
Visa: 800-847-2911

Embassies and Consulates
Australia: Australian High Commission, Bishop's Court Hill, St Michael, tel: 435-2834
Canada: Canadian High Commission, Bishop's Court Hill, St Michael, tel: 429-3550
United Kingdom: British High Commission, Lower Collymore Rock, St Michael, tel: 430-7800
United States: Embassy of the United States, Bridgetown, tel: 436-4950

Barbados Tourism Authority Offices

Barbados
Harbour Road, St Michael, tel: 246-427-2623

Abroad
United States
800 Second Avenue, NY, NY 10017, tel: 800-221-9831; 3440 Wilshire Blvd. Suite 1215, Los Angeles, CA 90010, tel: 213-380-2198
Canada
105 Adelaide Street West, Suite 1010, Toronto 214 9880, tel: 416-214 9882; 4800 de Maisonneuve W, Suite 532, Montreal, Quebec H3Z 1M2, tel: 514-932-3206
United Kingdom
263 Tottenham Court Road, London W1P 0LA, tel: 44-020-7-636-9448/9

FURTHER READING

Insight Guide: Barbados, Apa Publications, edited by Caroline Radula-Scott, 1999.
Simply Barbados, Sassman Publishing Co., Barbados. Annual read on local lifestyles.
A to Z of Barbadian Heritage (multiple authors), Jamaica, Heinemann Publishers (Caribbean Ltd.), 1990.
The Barbados Garrison and its Buildings, Warren Alleyne & Jill Sheppard, London, Macmillan Publishers Ltd, 1990.

Index

ACKNOWLEDGMENTS

Photography
15, 20, 34T, 42, 43, 45, 47T, 48, 52, Roxan Kinas
62T, 62B, 65, 67T, 71T, 76T,
76B, 81, 86, 89
8/9, 16, 23B, 24T, 26T, 26B, 28, 29, Martin Rosefeldt
33, 34B, 36, 37T, 38, 39T, 40, 44T,
46, 47B, 56, 64, 66B, 67B, 70B,
72, 73, 74T, 75T, 78T, 80, 90
71B Wolfgang Rössig
57 Mike Toy
2/3, 14, 21, 22, 23T, 24B, 25, 27, 30, Bill Wassman
31T, 31B, 32, 37B, 39B, 41, 42B, 44B,
49T, 49B, 50, 55, 58B, 60, 61, 63,
66T, 68, 69T, 69B, 70T, 74B, 75B,
77B, 78B, 83T, 83B, 84B, 85, 88T

Production Editor Mohammed Dar
Cover Bill Wassman
Cover Design Derrick Lim
Cartography Berndtson & Berndtson

Insight Guides

Alaska
Alsace
Amazon Wildlife
American Southwest
Amsterdam
Argentina
Atlanta
Athens
Australia
Austria
Bahamas
Bali
Baltic States
Bangkok
Barbados
Barcelona
Bay of Naples
Beijing
Belgium
Belize
Berlin
Bermuda
Boston
Brazil
Brittany
Brussels
Budapest
Buenos Aires
Burgundy
Burma (Myanmar)
Cairo
Calcutta
California
Canada
Caribbean
Catalonia
Channel Islands
Chicago
Chile
China
Cologne
Continental Europe
Corsica
Costa Rica
Crete
Crossing America
Cuba
Cyprus
Czech & Slovak
   Republics
Delhi, Jaipur, Agra
Denmark

Dresden
Dublin
Düsseldorf
East African Wildlife
East Asia
Eastern Europe
Ecuador
Edinburgh
Egypt
Finland
Florence
Florida
France
Frankfurt
French Riviera
Gambia & Senegal
Germany
Glasgow
Gran Canaria
Great Barrier Reef
Great Britain
Greece
Greek Islands
Hamburg
Hawaii
Hong Kong
Hungary
Iceland
India
India's Western
   Himalaya
Indian Wildlife
Indonesia
Ireland
Israel
Istanbul
Italy
Jamaica
Japan
Java
Jerusalem
Jordan
Kathmandu
Kenya
Korea
Lisbon
Loire Valley
London
Los Angeles
Madeira
Madrid
Malaysia
Mallorca & Ibiza
Malta

Marine Life in the
   South China Sea
Melbourne
Mexico
Mexico City
Miami
Montreal
Morocco
Moscow
Munich
Namibia
Native America
Nepal
Netherlands
New England
New Orleans
New York City
New York State
New Zealand
Nile
Normandy
Northern California
Northern Spain
Norway
Oman & the UAE
Oxford
Old South
Pacific Northwest
Pakistan
Paris
Peru
Philadelphia
Philippines
Poland
Portugal
Prague
Provence
Puerto Rico
Rajasthan
Rhine
Rio de Janeiro
Rockies
Rome
Russia
St Petersburg
San Francisco
Sardinia
Scotland
Seattle
Sicily
Singapore
South Africa
South America
South Asia

South India
South Tyrol
Southeast Asia
Southeast Asia Wildlife
Southern California
Southern Spain
Spain
Sri Lanka
Sweden
Switzerland
Sydney
Taiwan
Tenerife
Texas
Thailand
Tokyo
Trinidad & Tobago
Tunisia
Turkey
Turkish Coast
Tuscany
Umbria
US National Parks East
US National Parks West
Vancouver
Venezuela
Venice
Vienna
Vietnam
Wales
Washington DC
Waterways of Europe
Wild West
Yemen

Insight Pocket Guides

Aegean Islands★
Algarve★
Alsace
Amsterdam★
Athens★
Atlanta★
Bahamas★
Baja Peninsula★
Bali★
Bali Bird Walks
Bangkok★
Barbados★
Barcelona★
Bavaria★
Beijing★
Berlin★
Bermuda★